The Aporia of Unnamed Things

Poems, Drawings and illustrations

Tendai Rinos Mwanaka

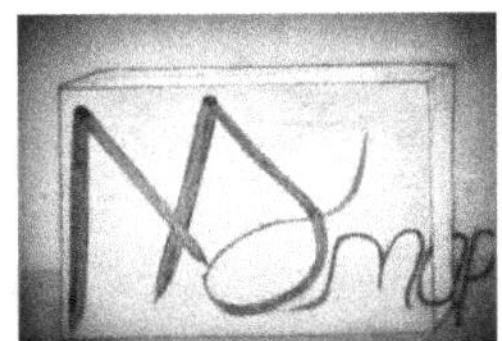

Mwanaka Media and Publishing Pvt Ltd,
Chitungwiza, Zimbabwe
*
Creativity, Wisdom, and Beauty

Publisher: *Mmap*
Mwanaka Media and Publishing Pvt Ltd
24 Svosve Road, Zengeza 1
Chitungwiza, Zimbabwe
mwanaka@yahoo.com
mwanaka13@gmail.com
https://www.mmapublishing.org
www.africanbookscollective.com/publishers/mwanaka-media-and-publishing
https://facebook.com/MwanakaMediaAndPublishing/

Distributed in and outside N. America by African Books Collective
orders@africanbookscollective.com
www.africanbookscollective.com

ISBN: 978-1-77933-143-4
EAN: 9781779331434

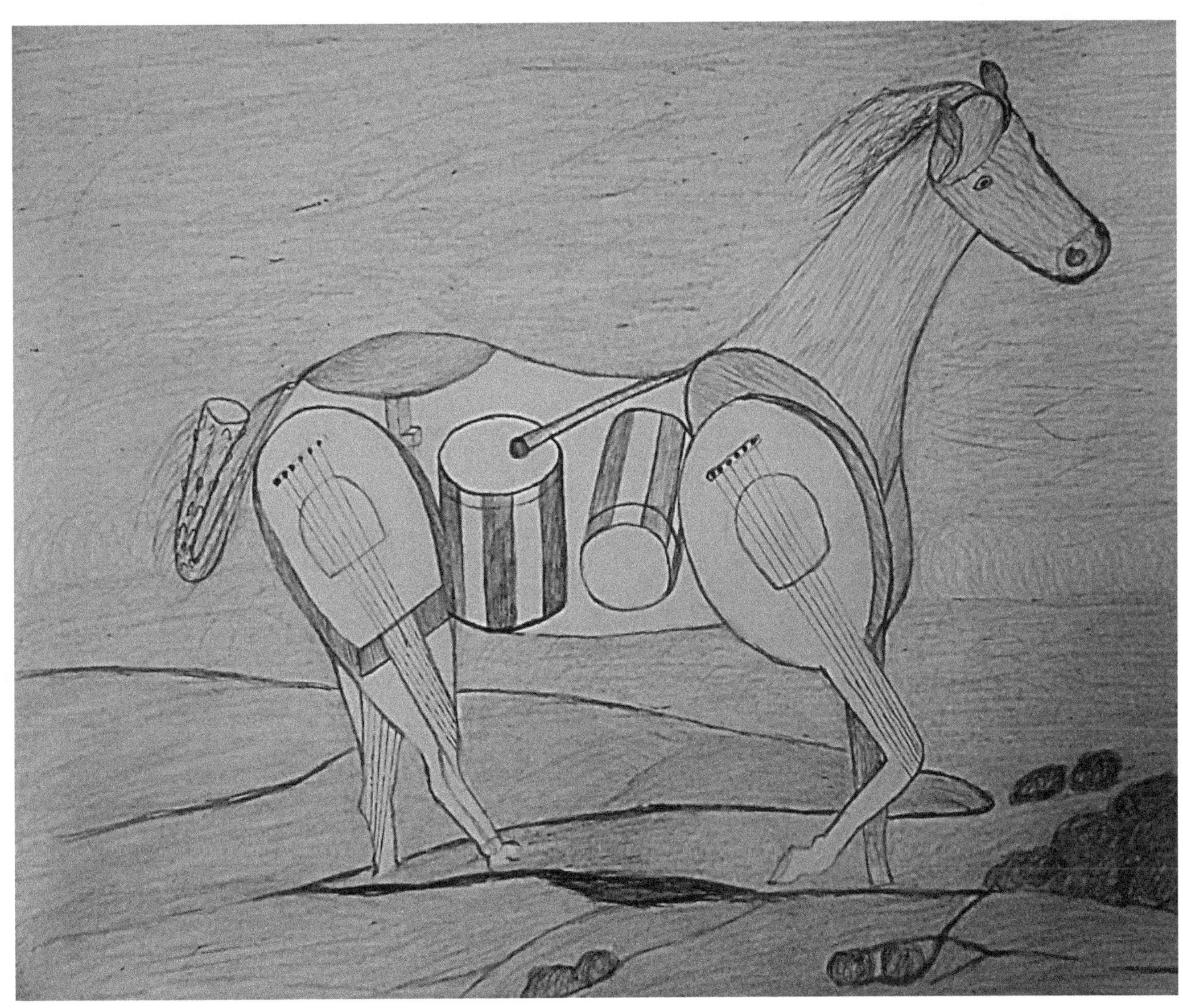

~~Unnamed 1~~
Mediums: graphite and colour pencils on paper
Size: A3
Year: 2018

The guitar strums,
Thumping drums
Echoing
Ruminating saxophones
in starless skies
Stomping shakers,
percussions,
Percussive,
sea waves on black sea rocks
The musical horse that rocks
that line that divides,
of rock and soft, earths

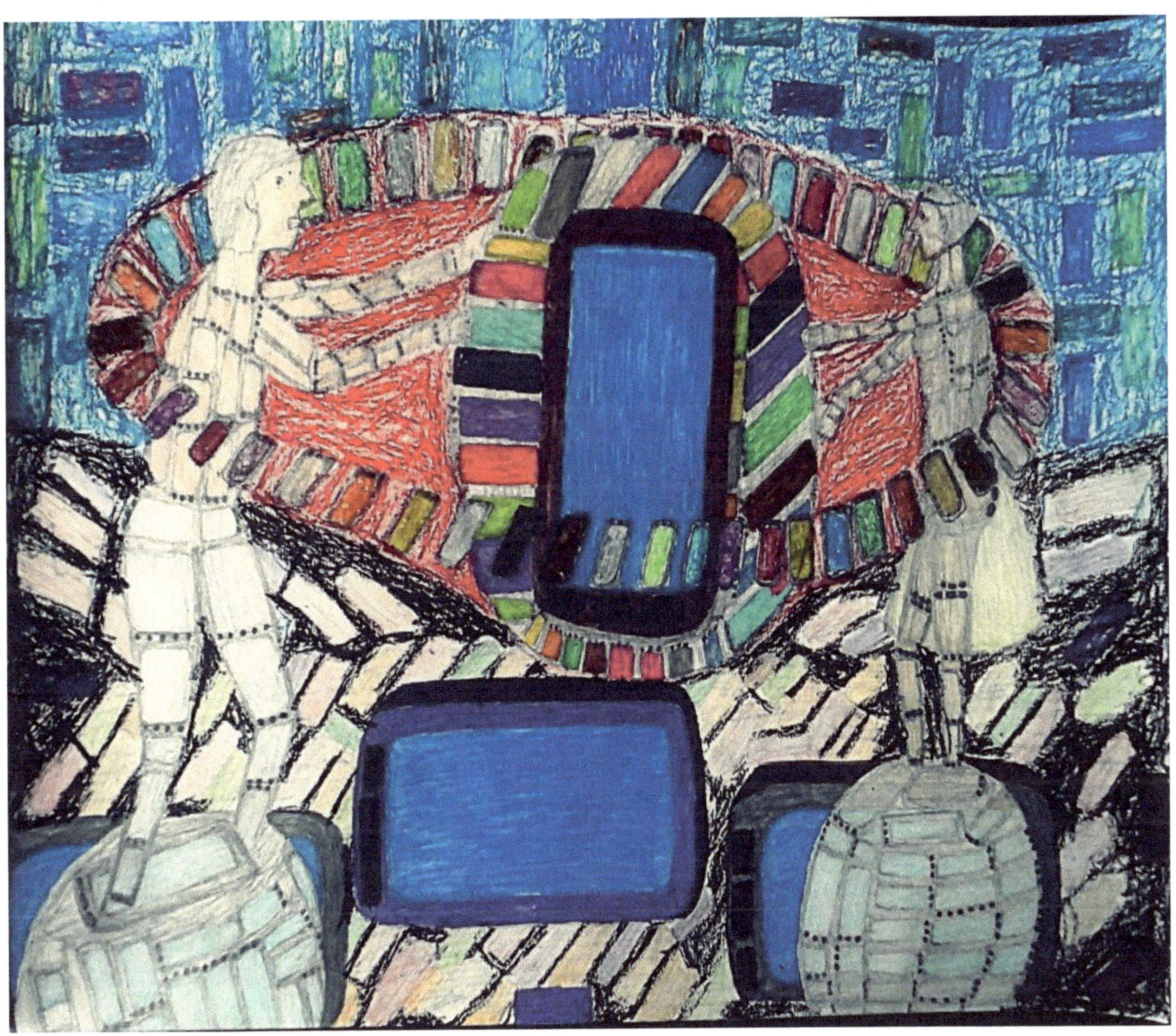

~~Unnamed 2~~
Mediums: graphite, color pencils, fibre ink, oil pastels on paper
Size: A3
Year 2018

Machine fantasies
Are new fancies
at the tips of our swiping fingers
That soft touch that once lingered,
Between human and human,
thing and a thing...
is now a chasm
to two hearts chanting
for each other?

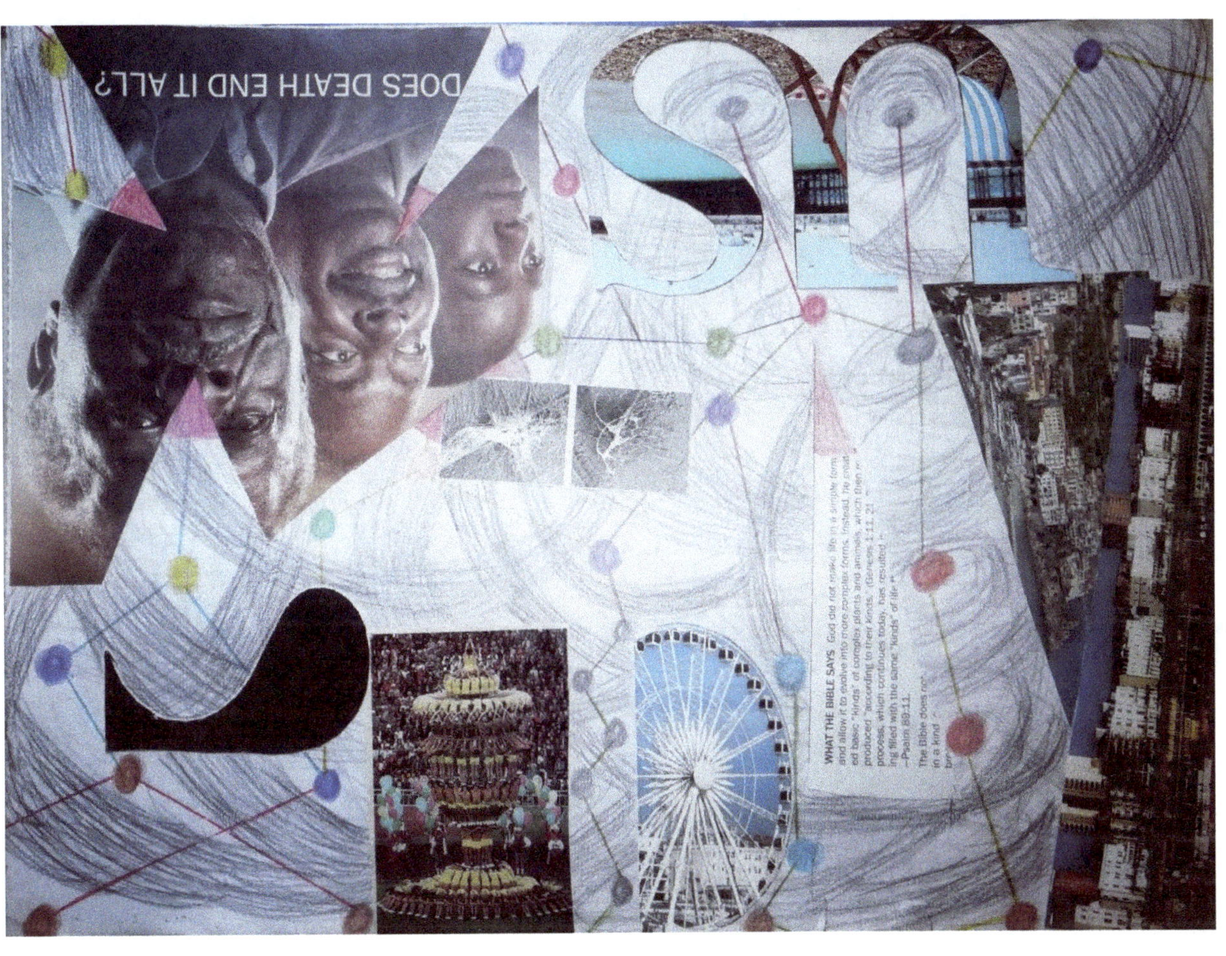
DOES DEATH END IT ALL?
WHAT THE BIBLE SAYS

~~Unnamed 3~~
Mediums: collages, graphite, colour pencils on paper
Size: A3
Year: 2021

Every time I hear the words
Is every time there are harsh words
Every time I see the looks
Is every time there are sneers, jeers
Every time they say they don't see colours
Is every time they see the colours
Every time they complain
they are tired of hearing about it
Is every time I hear of humans
Tired of another human's humanity,
Is every time I want to ask,
does death end it all?

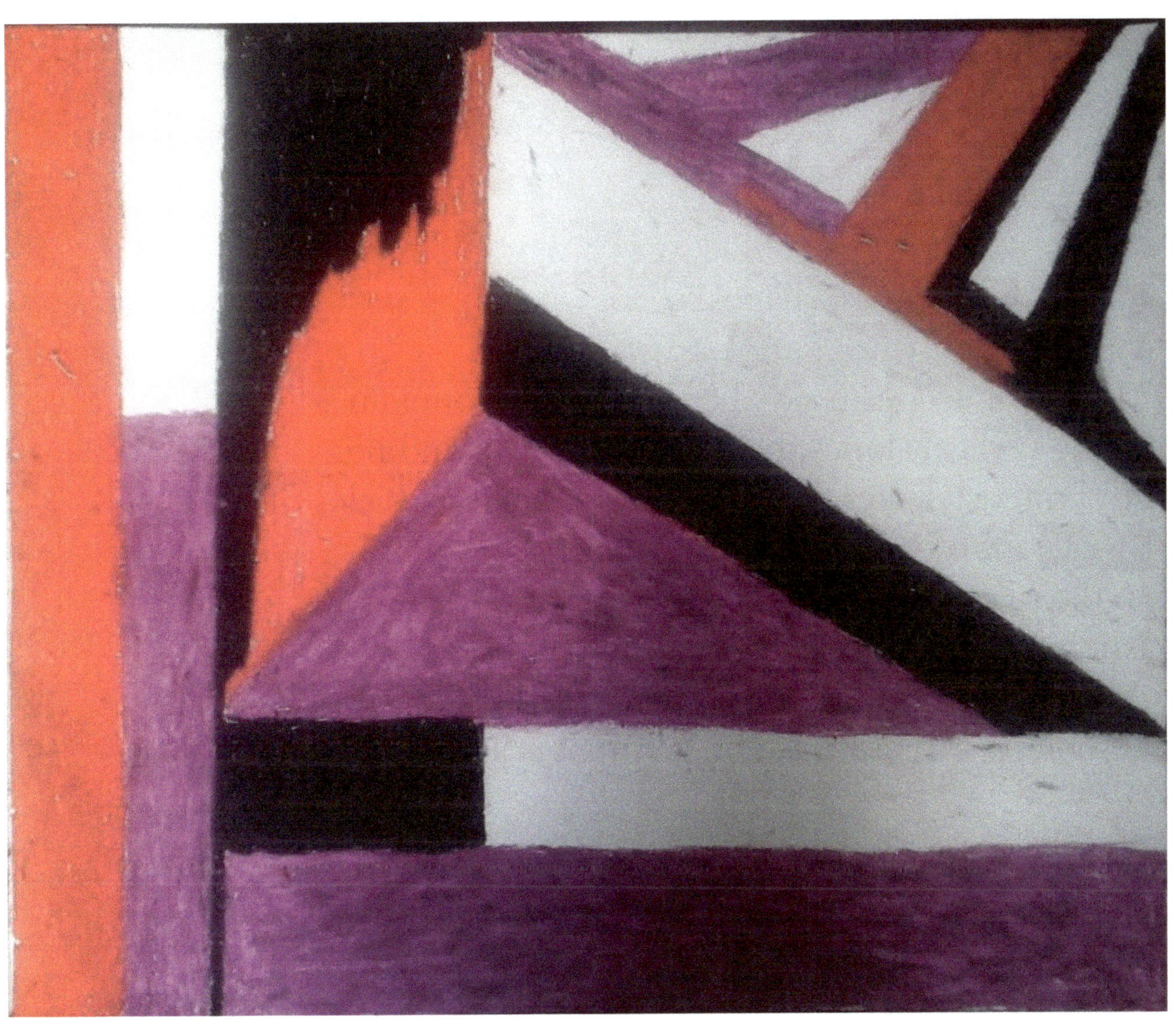

~~Unnamed 4~~
Mediums: oil pastels on paper
Size: A3
Year: 2018

Planes, lines, lanes, shapes...
White, black, purple, red...
My guessing cousin says he is seeing a mountain
In the vertical slopes that separates black and red
And my sister says she is seeing triangular cubicles of
Purple rain, purple rain, purple rain...
In the music the triangle fails to contain
And my lover says she sees white rectangles
And angular white clouds tagging her heart
"Honie, is this artwork about you, it is about us?"

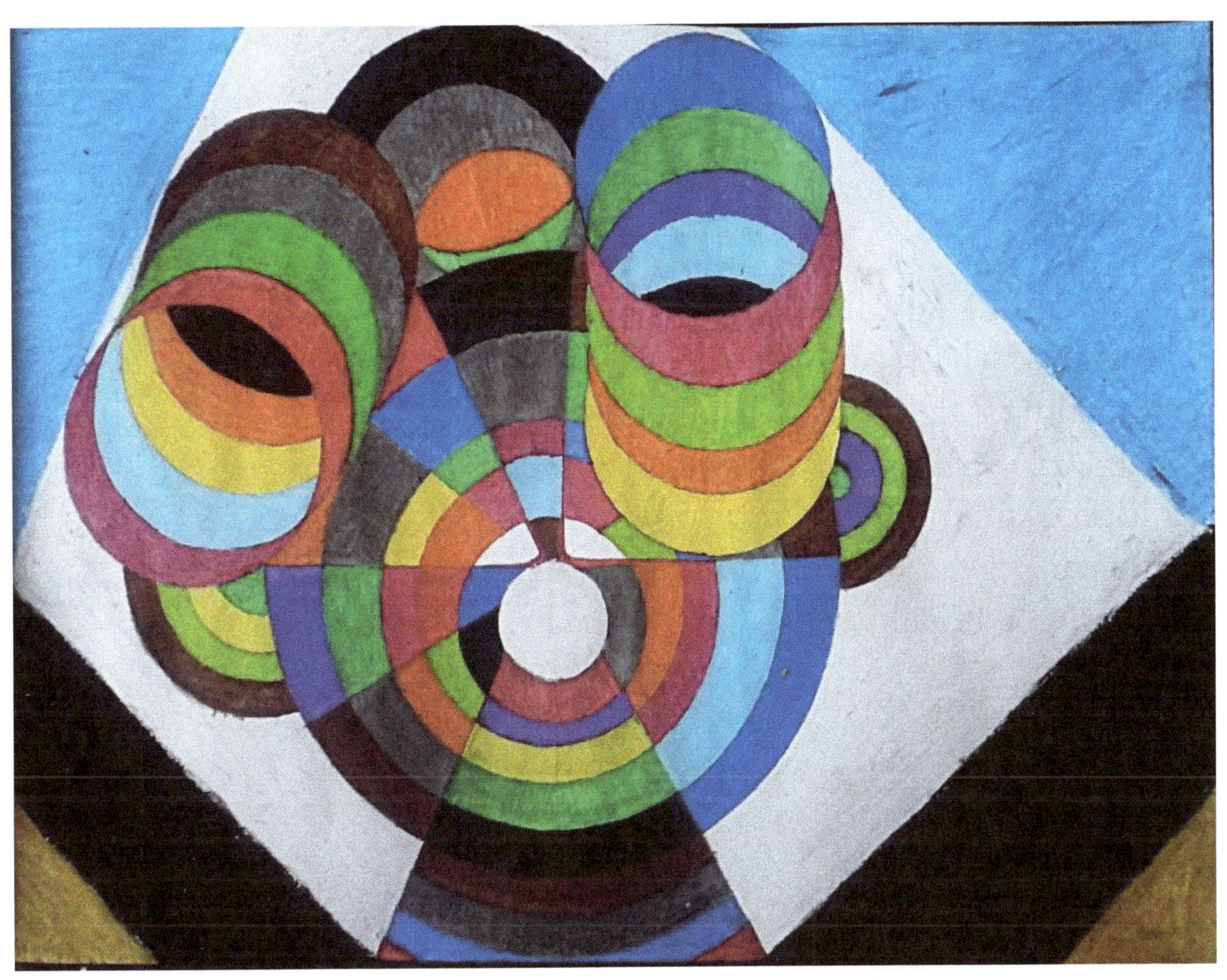

~~Unnamed 5~~
Mediums: fibre ink, pastels on paper
Size: A3
Year: 2018

Enigma in the far-off 1990s, *Eyes of Truth*
Like Enya, who hasn't *returned to innocence*
In the almost decade she has been mute
Since 2015's *Dark Silk Island,* after *the winter had come*
Coldplay came with pinging interludes in *Mylo Xyloto*
Before the *head that was full of dreams* emptied me out.
And now, I am all *yellow*

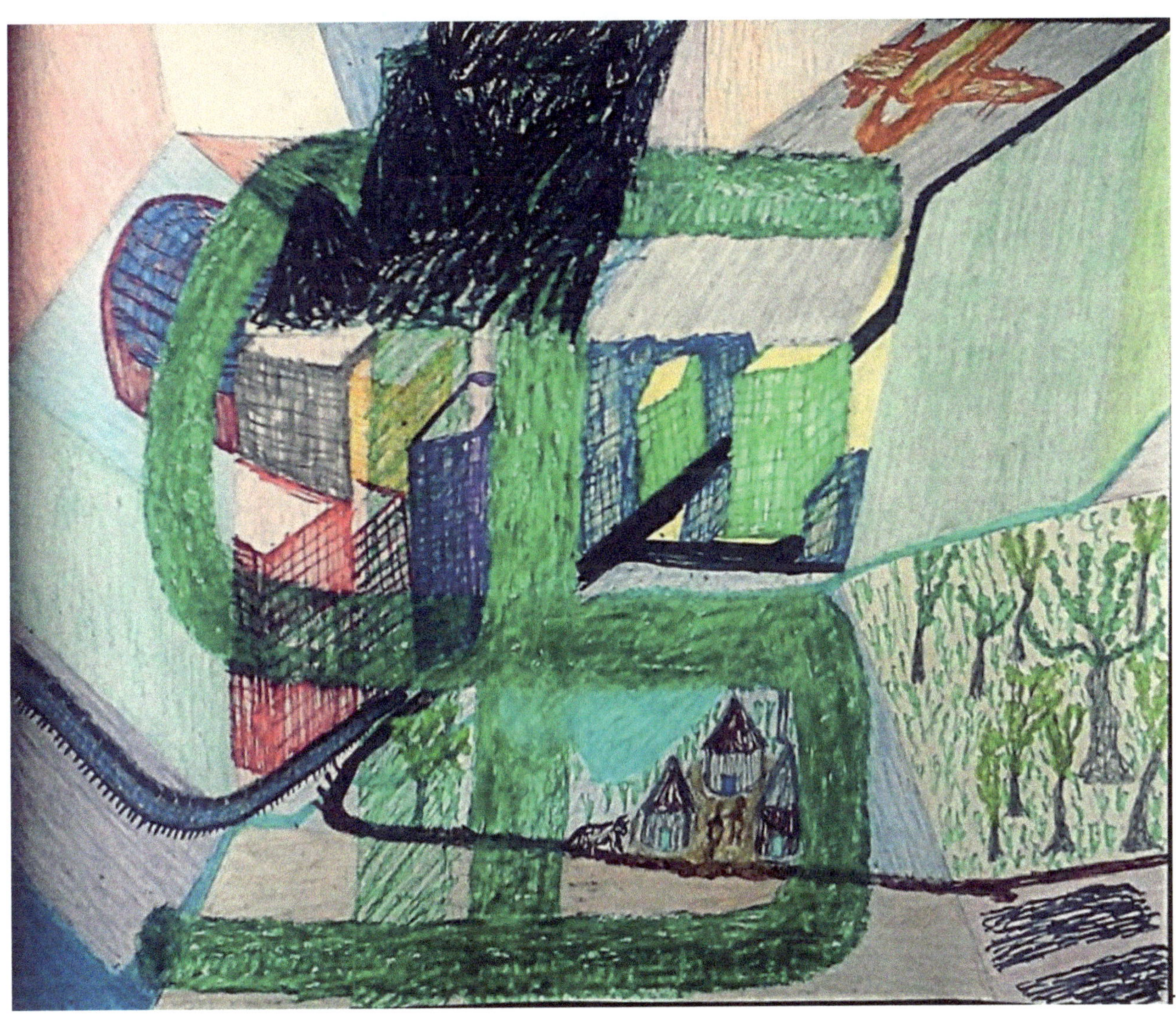

~~Unnamed 6~~
Mediums: fibre ink, oil pastels on paper
Size: A3
Year: 2018

Sleeping on a reed mat in a green ~~dollar~~ sign
In an African hut, in the middle of the savannas,
In the far off conurbations of winding ~~dollar~~ signs
In trains that circles it, roads that form cooked spaghetti shapes
The petrol ~~dollar~~ fuels the huts, metropolis, farm, caves
Of the humming, huffing, puffing- sweat, pain, bleeding veins
That are in a prayer to their real God, they pray every day to,
To feed the fat cats angels of the petrol ~~dollar~~ nation

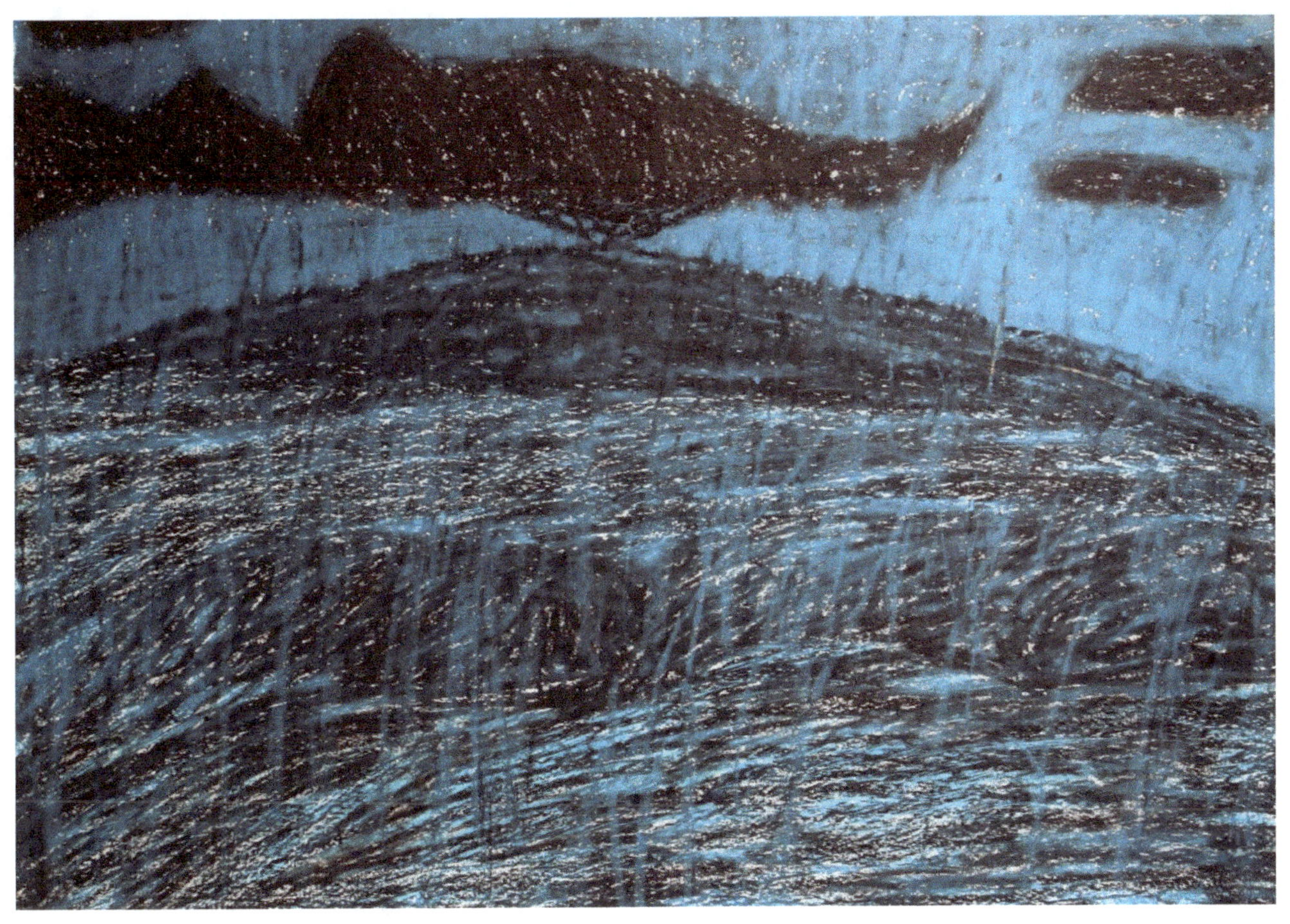

~~Unnamed 7~~
Mediums: oil pastels on paper
Size: A3
Year: 2018

Somewhere in the dark blanket soul
of the night's skies
Somewhere where a thought caresses
That line that separates
sea's waters and night's skies
Are some blackened thought lines,
Some big and some small splotches
Shapes that lurches and lounges
on this bluesy soul

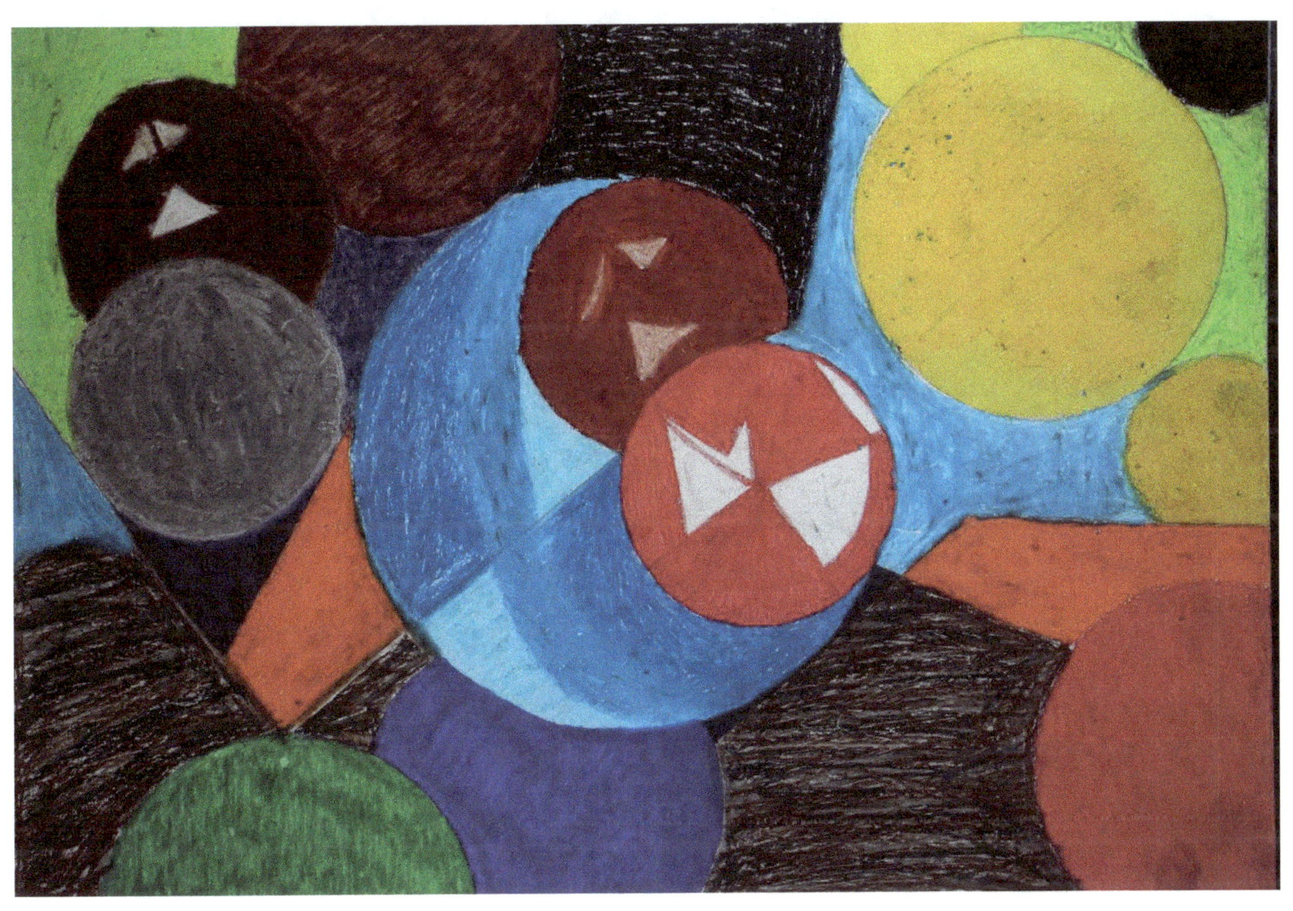

~~Unnamed 8~~

Mediums: fibre ink and oil pastels on paper
Size: A3
Year: 2018

Circles of colours rolling their bodies
To the east, west, south, north...
Into the skies
To upraise the bodies
Into the spaces
Of circles of ambition
forming human bodies,
limbs, eyes, thought, patterns
Propelling us to our intents

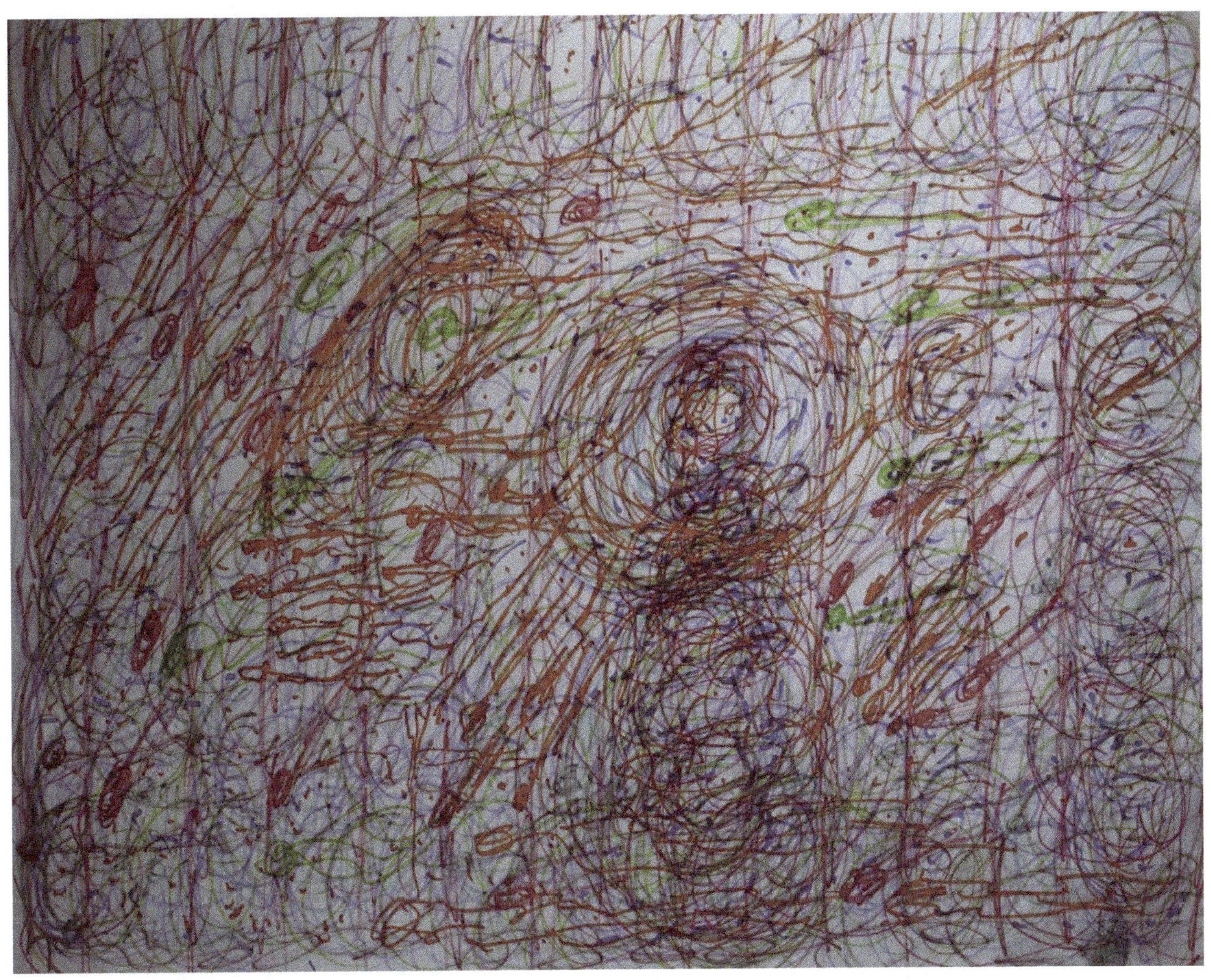

~~Unnamed 9~~
Mediums: fibre ink on paper
Size: A3
Year: 2019

The hand that calculates the noise of the traffics
In Lillian Ngoyi street as the earthbound birds
Flies into a city he has failed to call home
The hand that estimates the shrieking cries of a new born
Trying to identify the colours of the new world of noise
He or she, or they, them didn't volunteer to enter into
The hand that interprets the exasperated cooing sounds
of mother-hen, trying to hem the cries down, lower them down
And the mother before mother-hen's admonishments and advice
To the hand that fails to tell of what eats this hand
The hand that fails to hear the sounds that do not sound
Into the depths, ventricles, joints, nail roots of this hand

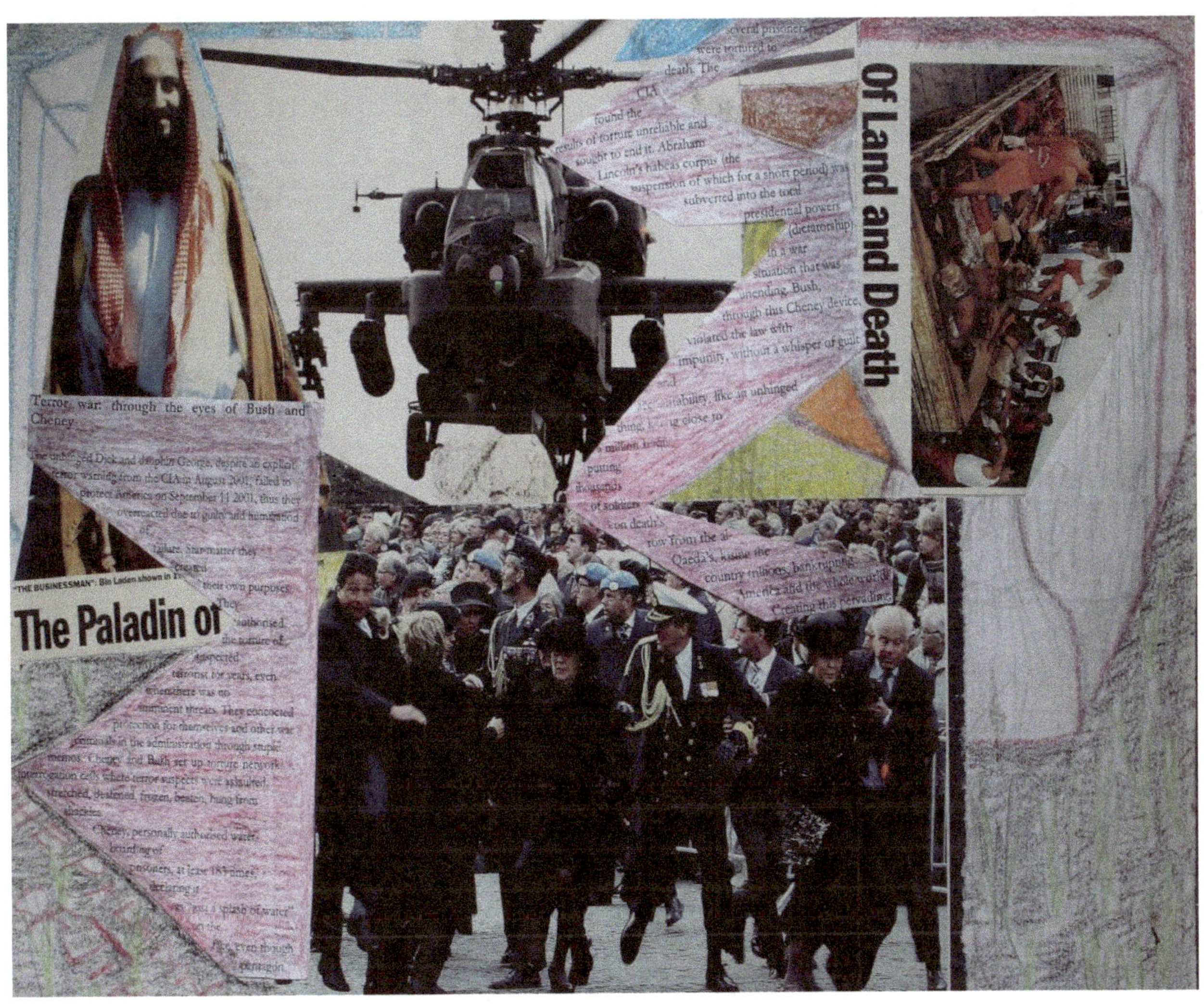

Terror war: through the eyes of Bush and Cheney
protect America on September 11 2001, thus they
"THE BUSINESSMAN": Bin Laden shown in
The Paladin of
their own purposes.
They
authorised
the torture of
suspected
terrorist for years, even
imminent threats. They concocted
protection for themselves and other war
criminals in the administration through stupid
memos. Cheney and Bush set up torture network
interrogation cells where terror suspects were assaulted,
stretched, deafened, frozen, beaten, hung from
shackles.
Cheney personally authorised water-
boarding of
prisoners, at least 183 times,
declaring it
just a splash of water"
even though
pentagon
several prisoners
were tortured to
death. The
CIA
found the
results of torture unreliable and
sought to end it. Abraham
Lincoln's habeas corpus (the
suspension of which for a short period) was
subverted into the total
presidential powers
(dictatorship)
in a war
situation that was
unending. Bush,
through this Cheney device,
violated the law with
impunity, without a whisper of guilt
like an unhinged
putting
thousands
of soldiers
on death's
row from the al
Qaeda's
country trillions, bankrupting
America and the whole world.
Creating this pervading
Of Land and Death

~~Unnamed 10~~
Mediums: graphite, oil pastels, collages, printed poem on paper
Size: A3
Year: 2021

Through Osama bin laden's grey-whitey fingers
That rocks the head of death
Through Bush, Chaney
And Blair's all mongering eyes of war
That's how we have danced to this acid rain
Like Gene Kelly *in the Rain*
Dancin in the rain
Da da da da da da
And the *Boom, boom, boom, boom....*
We have come to call the paladin Jihad!

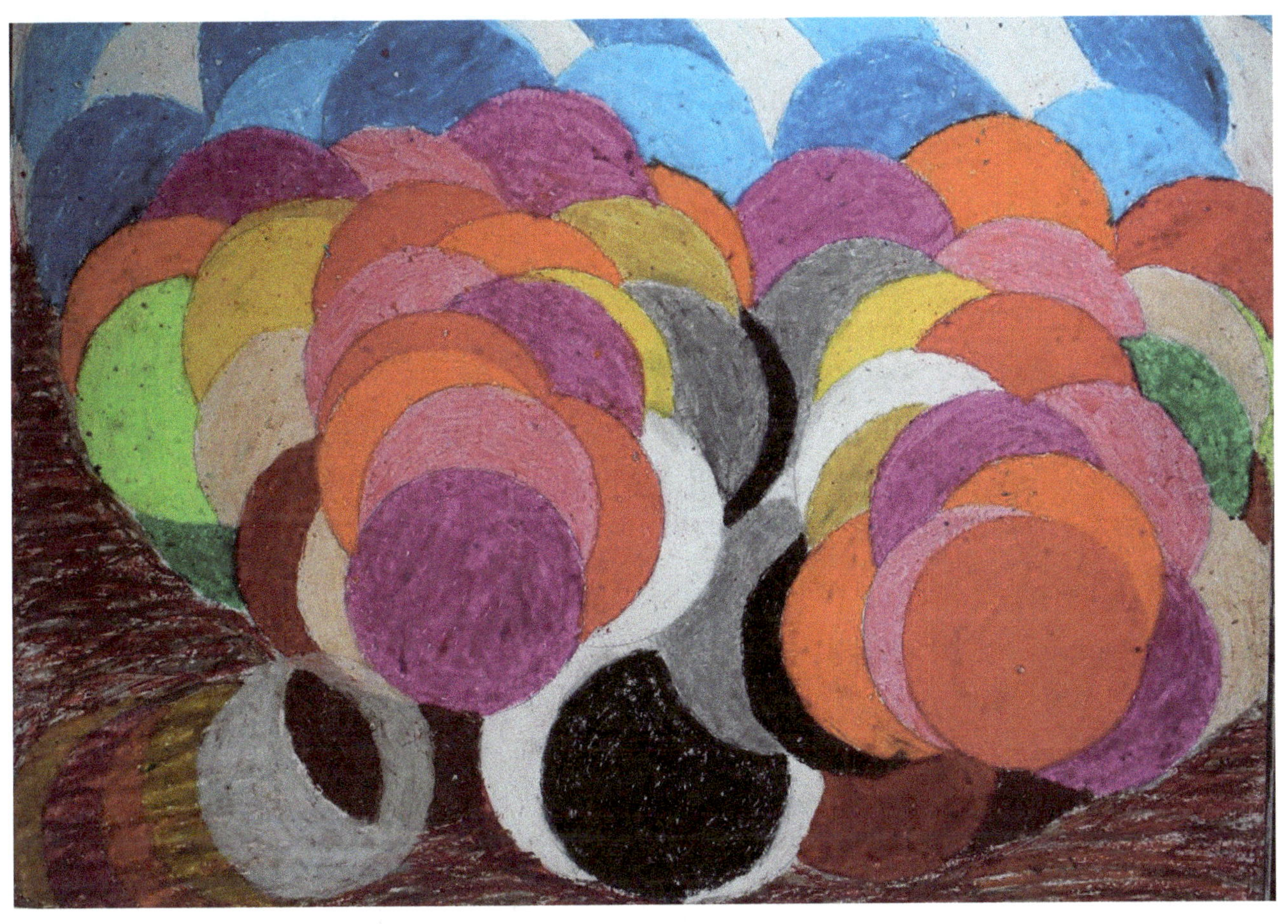

~~Unnamed 11~~

Mediums: graphite, oil pastels, collages, printed poem on paper
Size: A3
Year: 2020

a circle for femininity,
a circle for totality,
a symbol of the sun, moon, wholeness, origin, perfection,
a circle of the self, soul, infinite, eternity, timelessness
a circle for cyclical movements,
a circle of moving on
a circle for G.O.D
a D.O.G with no centre
whose circumference is nowhere
a circle for evil spirits whispering, whimpering...
circular forms that leads to sacrificial rocks, pagan beliefs...
a circle for human imperfections, bile of hurt, infinite swing of the pendulum.
people who got the circles when the shapes were handed down,
a circle for destroyers of all virtues.
They are here and they were there.
When shapes were given, what shape were given to you?

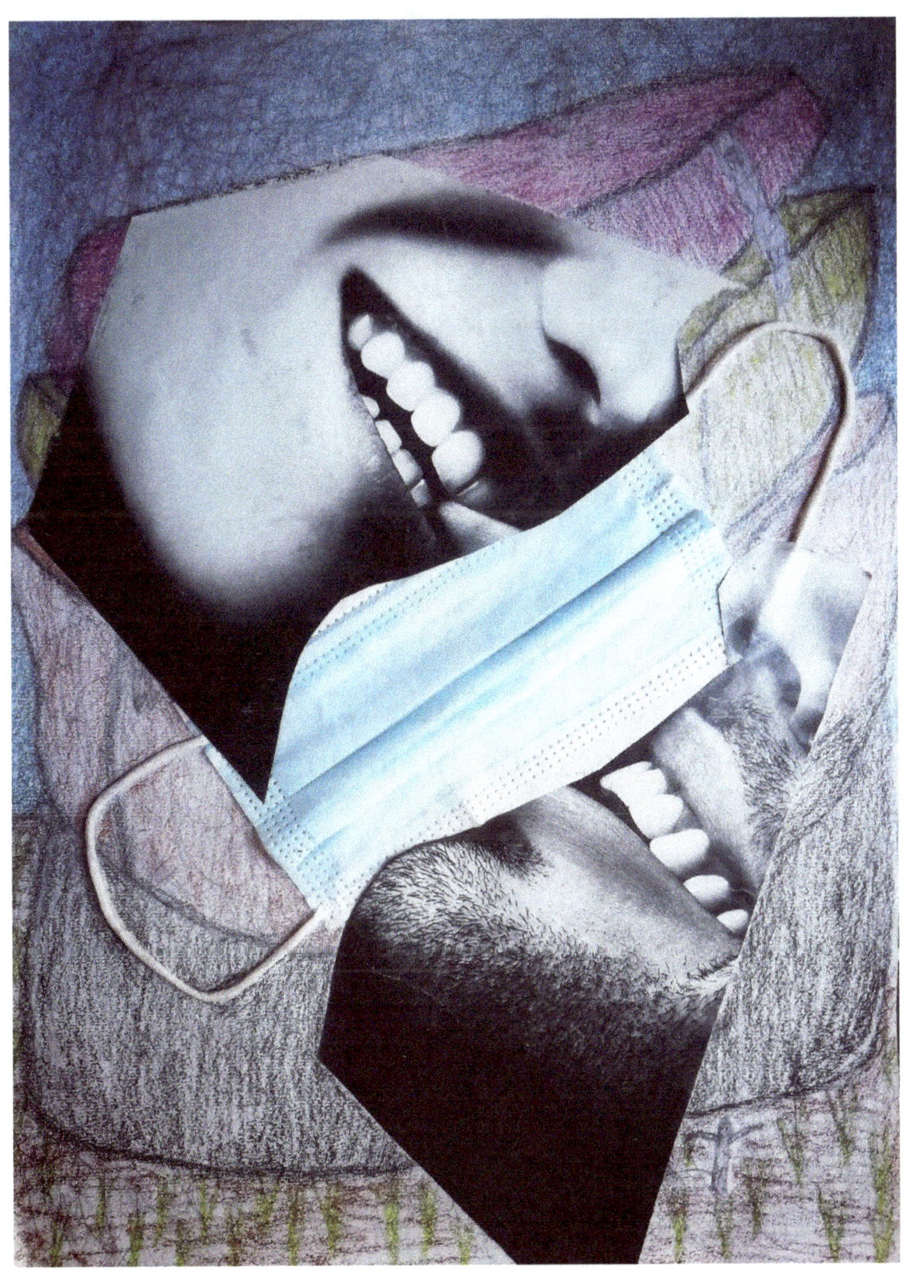

~~Unnamed 12~~
Mediums: graphite, oil pastels, collages on paper
Size: A3
Year: 2021

Darling you, even though I miss your kisses,
Please put your mask on
Darling you, make sure it covers your mouth
Putting the ring on it has to wait for another season
Darling you, the wedding cake will have to go
Or it will dry out before we have a date
Darling you, we will see each other
At the end of this lockdown, this lockdown, this lockdown...
Darling you, I miss your hugs, coos, breathing...
Your mouth's warm husk caressing my soft lips
Darling you, I miss your soft kisses,
Your teeth chewing my lips playfully

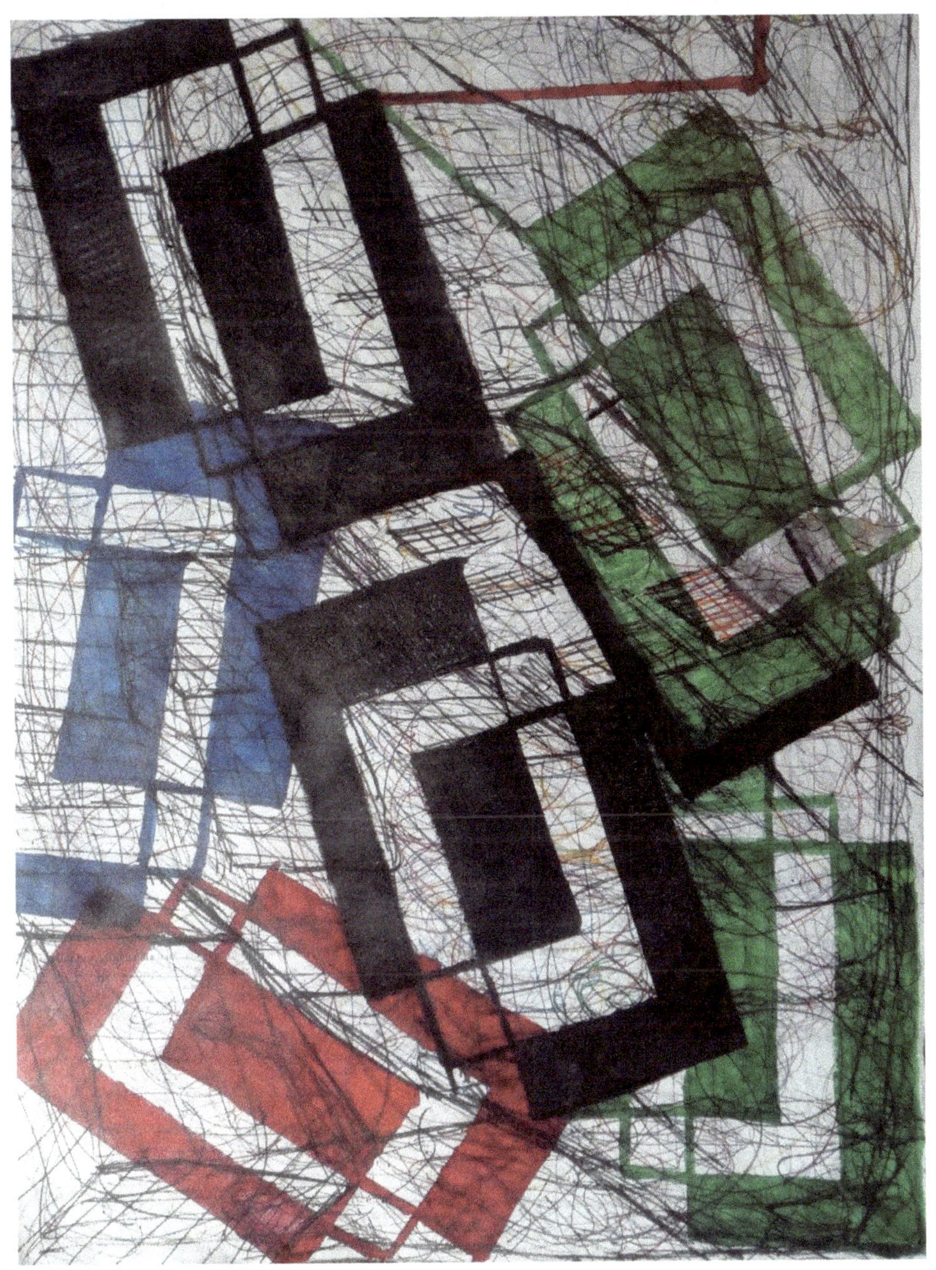

~~Unnamed 13~~
Mediums: pen ink and markers on paper
Size: A3
Year: 2020

Volume of planes
   Volume of the spaces
      Volume of boxes
         Volume of moving matter
            Volume of lines
               Volume of thoughts
                  Volume of volumes
Of that which we don't see
That which sees us

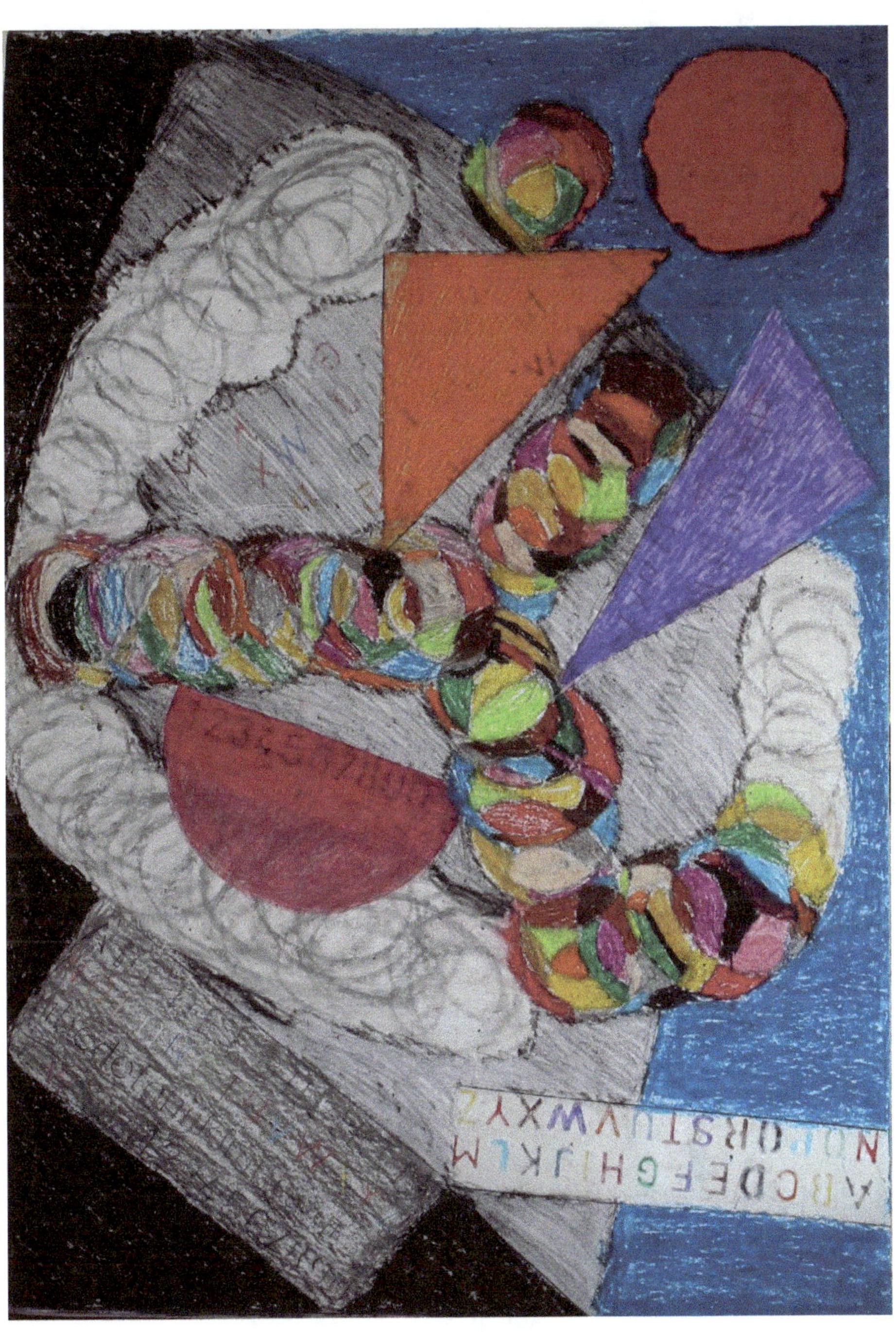
ABCDEFGHIJKLM
NOPQRSTUVWXYZ

~~Unnamed 14~~
Mediums: graphite, oil pastels, and fibre ink on paper
Size: A3
Year: 2018

Did the humans started by speaking the vowels *Aaa*
Eee, Iii, Ooo, Uuuu
By pronouncing Aaa as Aey,
Number one begins the numbering of things
Did the humans started at Ziii (Zeet), and go back
To Zero, Number nine is not the last number…
Is God then a number, unlike infinity?
If they started at Aey what letter is God then?
If they started at Zeet, why did they patch God Outside?
The naming alphabets and numbers?
Every day, we pray to memory loss
For if we knew his position on the alphabet
We would know where to send our noises
As our prayer-hands point to the universes
Trying to connect loss of memory and space
The failure of which we mistakenly call God?

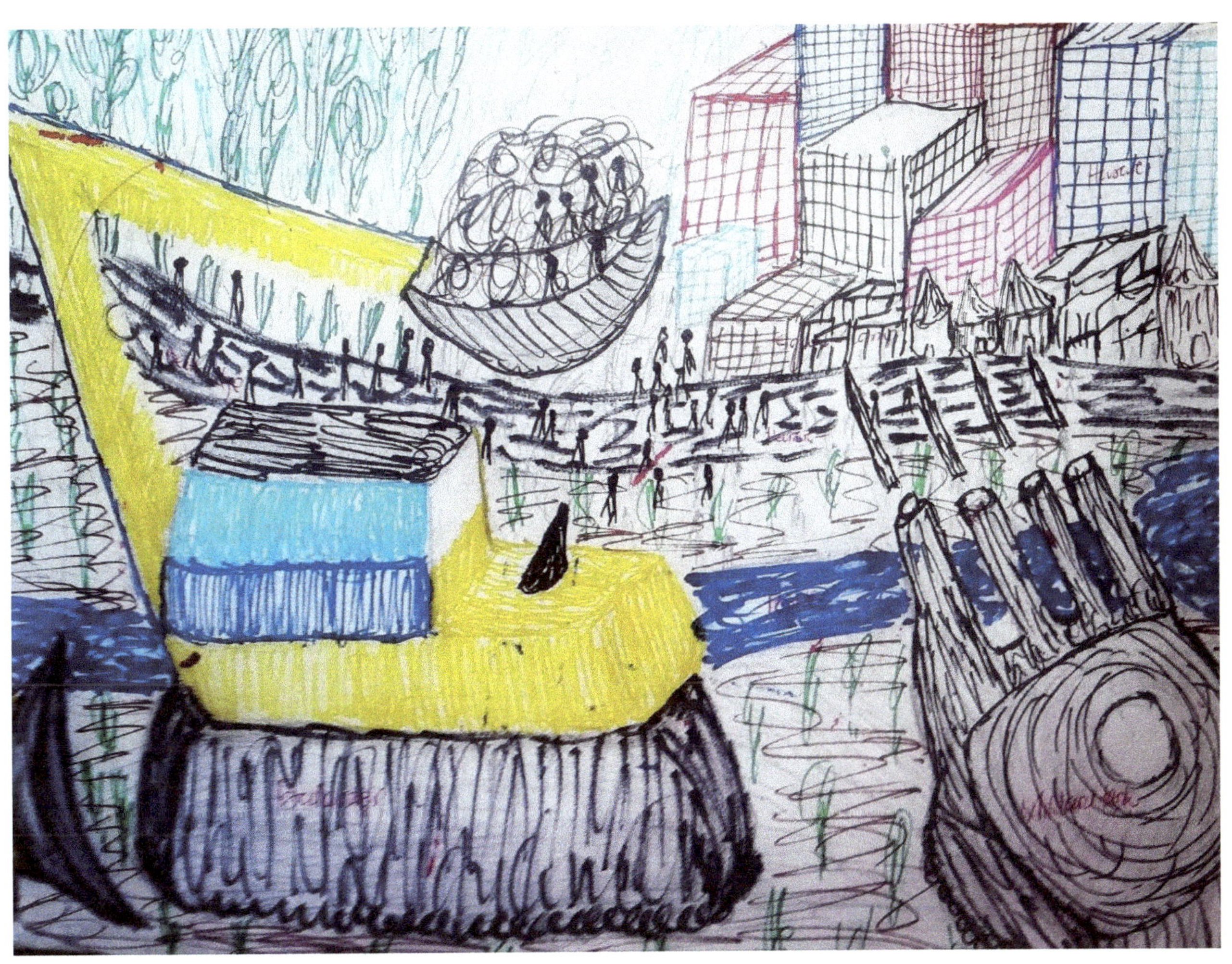

~~Unnamed 15~~
Mediums: graphite, fibre ink, markers on paper
Size: A3
Year: 2019

After the AK47's klaklakha dhudhudhu, the billowing red arrows flying in the city streets like the humans scurrying all over..., after the thunder of tanks in Nyerere street, after those graders that razed homes in St Mary's, after the button sticks on backs of striking teachers, after the stinking waters in the eyes and faces of opposition supporters, after the rubber bullets pelting and breaking the blood of our speeding shadows, after the removal of that old hulk at 1 Chancellor Road on an eventful day in November, after another round of voting, after the courts, the demonstrations, after rejecting the results...
And here we are again....

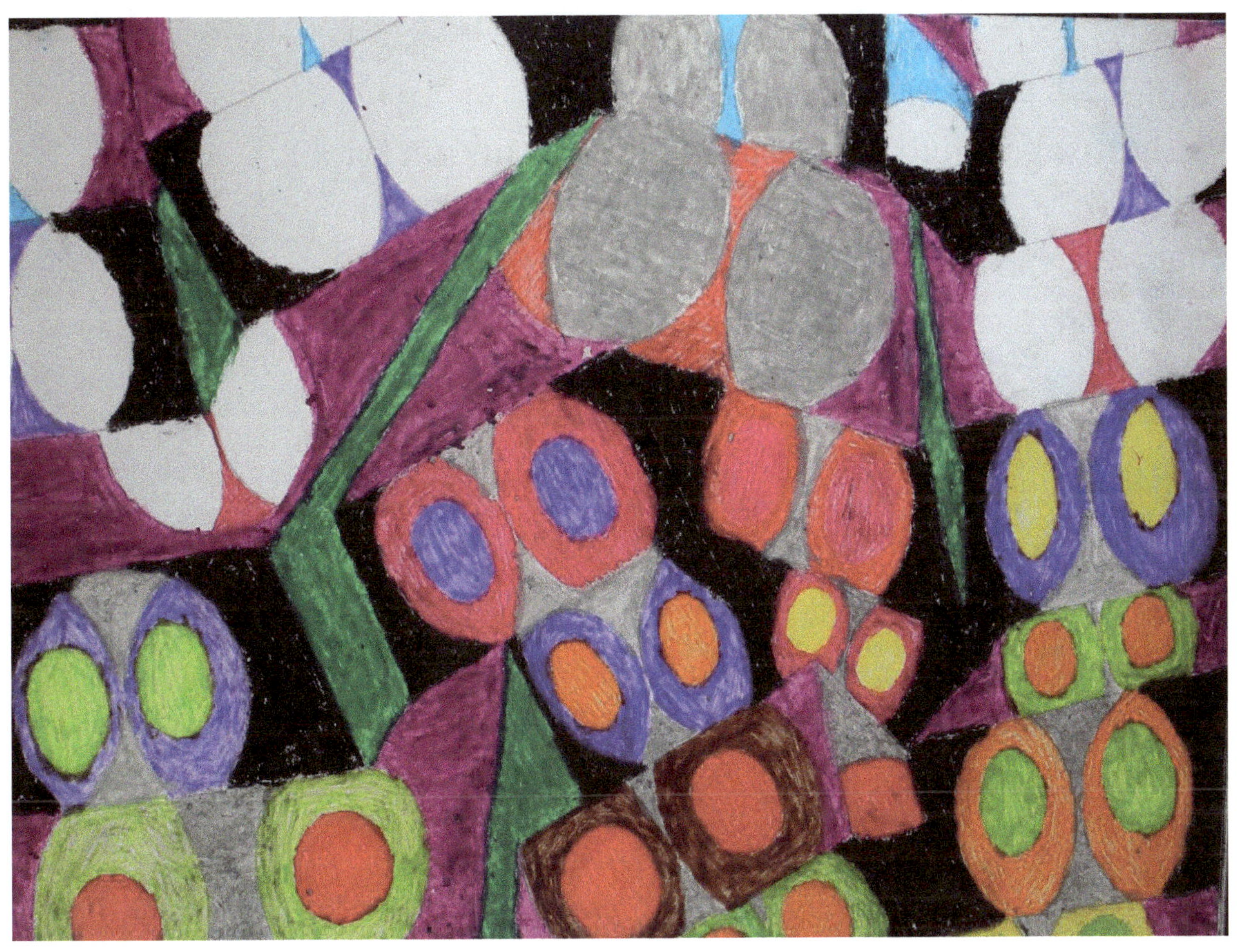

~~Unnamed 16~~
Mediums: graphite, oil pastels and fibre ink on paper
Size: A3
Year: 2019

Two by twos
Two towards
Two in union
Two is a contest
Two as a tapestry

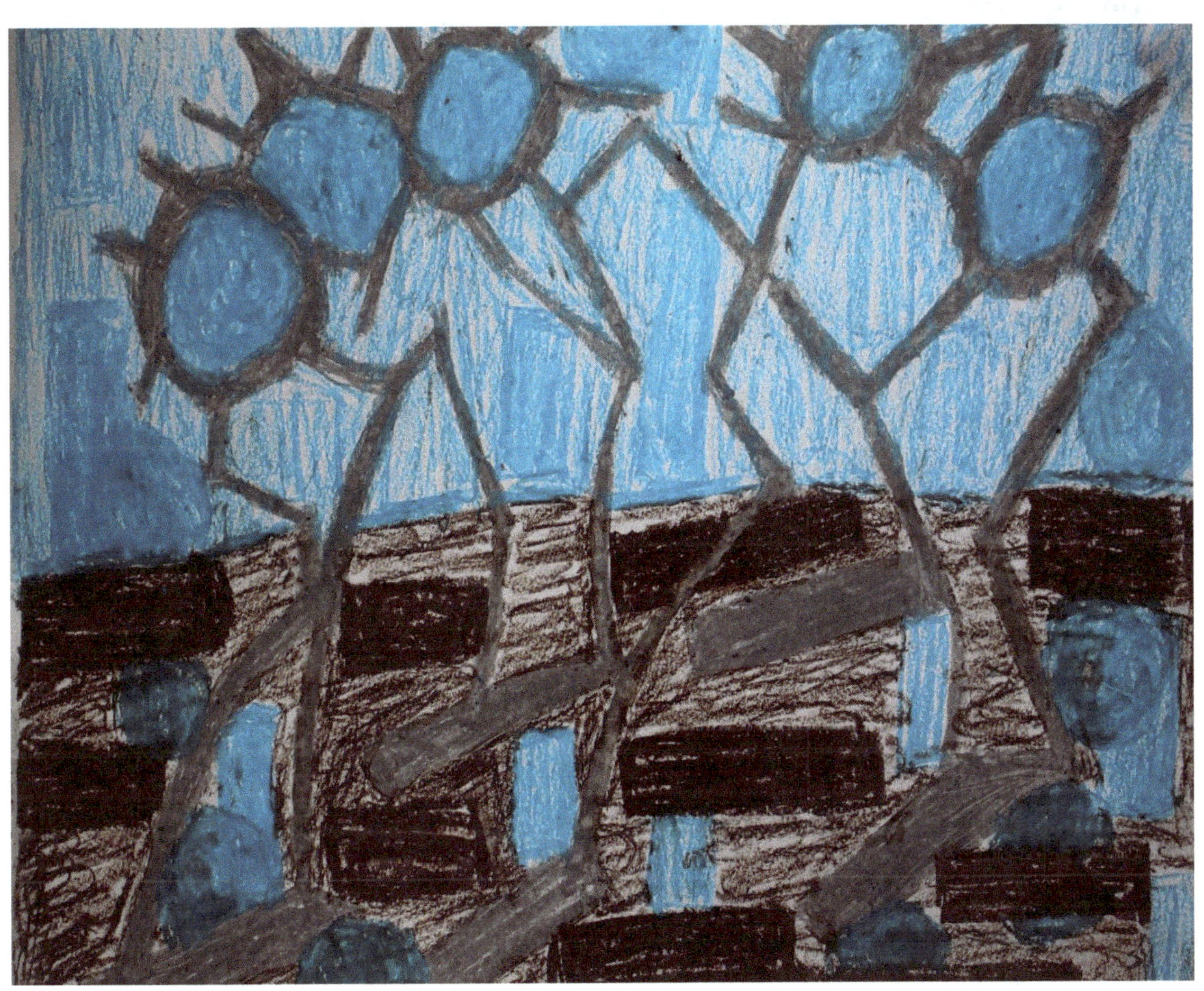

~~Unnamed 17~~
Mediums: oil pastels on paper
Size: A3
Year: 2019

Oneness
In community
Conversation
In Circularity
Comprehension
In universality
Whose wo/man
Whose Connection
Whose Cooperation
In stellar orbiting...

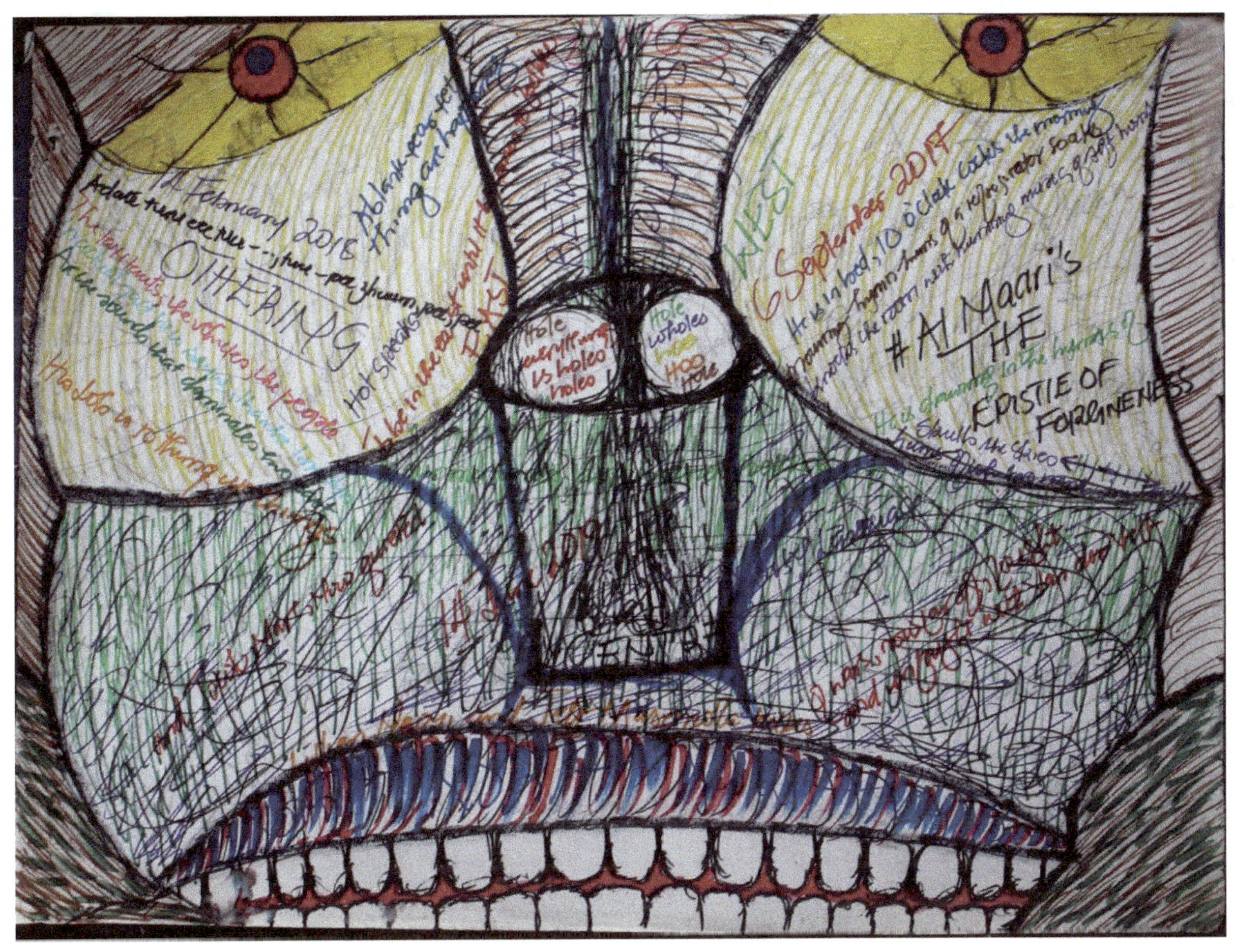
OTHERINGS
WEST
6 September 2017
#Al Maari's
THE
EPISTLE OF
FORGIVENESS
Hole
wholes

~~Unnamed 18~~
Mediums: graphite, markers, fibre pen ink and ballpoint pen ink on paper
Size: A3
Year: 2021

Job's job was to feel thimgs
To work through thimgs
To not have no choice
                Every day he felt thimgs
He couldn't stop feeling thimgs
                Everythimg were thimgs
He was a thimg
Everythimg were wounds, holes
He couldn't stop to thimg of thimgs
              That could make him whole,
Again, he had no choice!

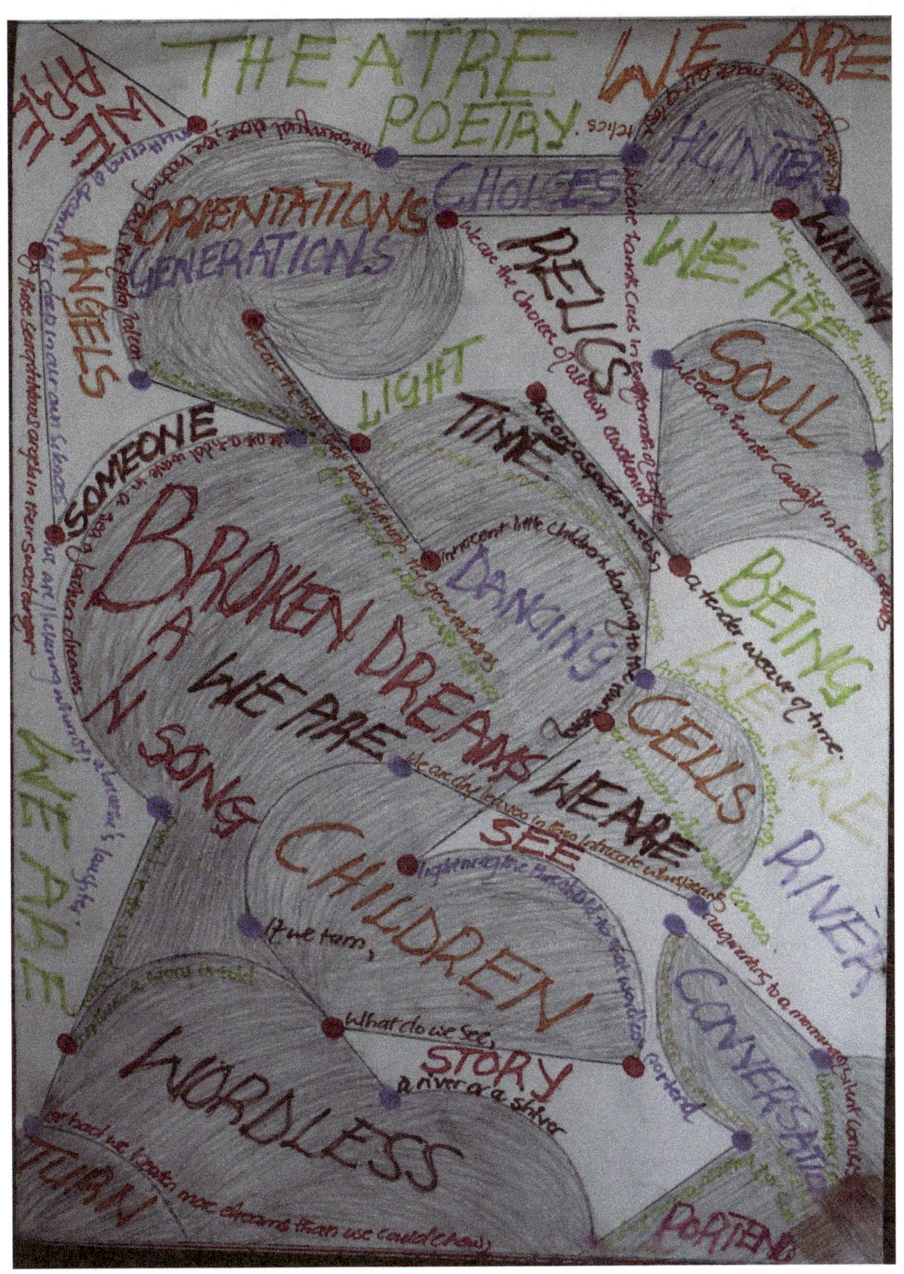
THEATRE
WE ARE
POETRY.
HUNTER
CHOICES
ORIENTATIONS
GENERATIONS
RELICS
WE ARE
WRITING
ANGELS
SOUL
LIGHT
TIME
SOMEONE
BROKEN DREAMS
DANCING
BEING
PAIN
WE ARE
CELLS
WE ARE
SONG
CHILDREN
SEE
RIVER
WE ARE
a tender weave of time.
If we turn,
What do we see,
STORY
a river or a shiver
WORDLESS
TURN
PORTEND

~~Unnamed 19~~
Mediums: graphite, fibre ink pen and ballpoint pen ink on paper
Size: A3
Year: 2019

~~We are these:~~
~~#cells, #this soul, #this being #choices of our own awakening #light that pours through the generations #Innocent little children dancing to the rain song #For a season of green to atone for our wrongs.~~

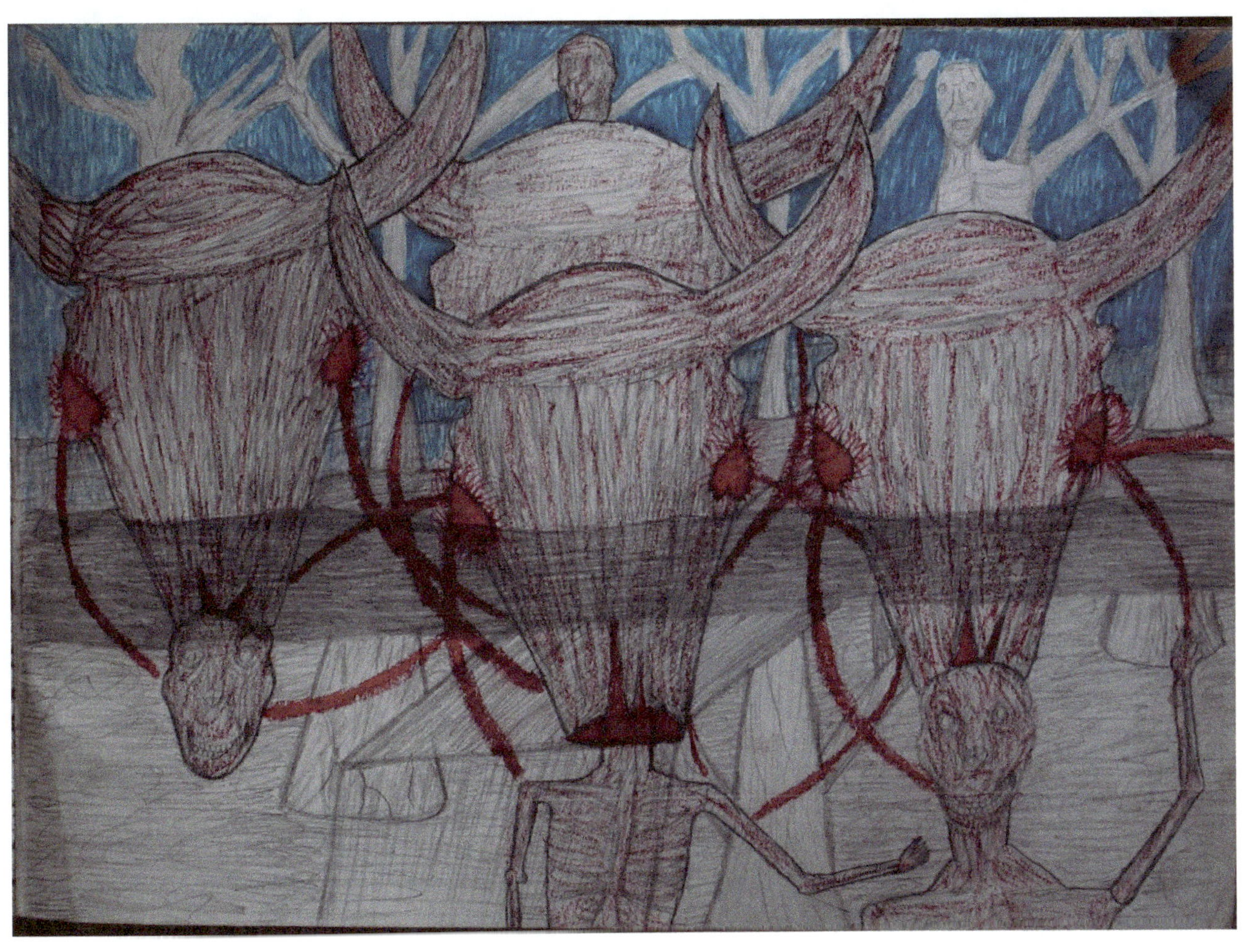

~~Unnamed 20~~
Mediums: graphite, oil pastels and ball point pen ink on paper
Size: A3
Year: 2021

....inner animals,
....inner spirits,
....inner universes,
....inner strata
Inner, inner, inner...
....percolating spirits

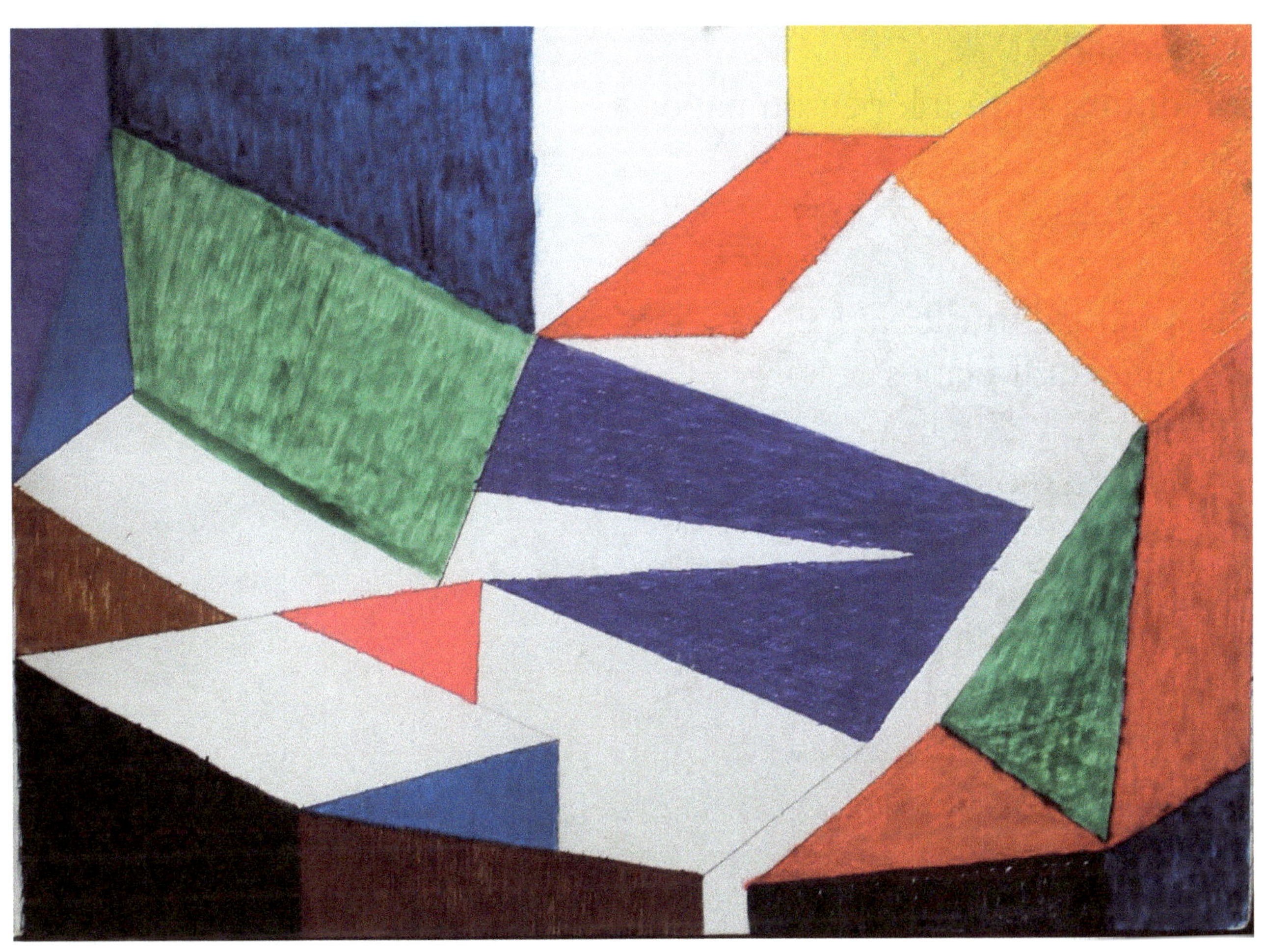

~~Unnamed 21~~
Mediums: fibre ink pen on paper
Size: A3
Year: 2021

In spherical music
Architectural planes
Plenary in volumes
In buildings of blue hues
In arches, reforming
In tangent lines asymmetrical
In Curvatures deepening
In triangular human noises
In angles of Lost Angeles
In rectangular silences,
In earths being boxed
Boxes in buildings
Bodies boxed

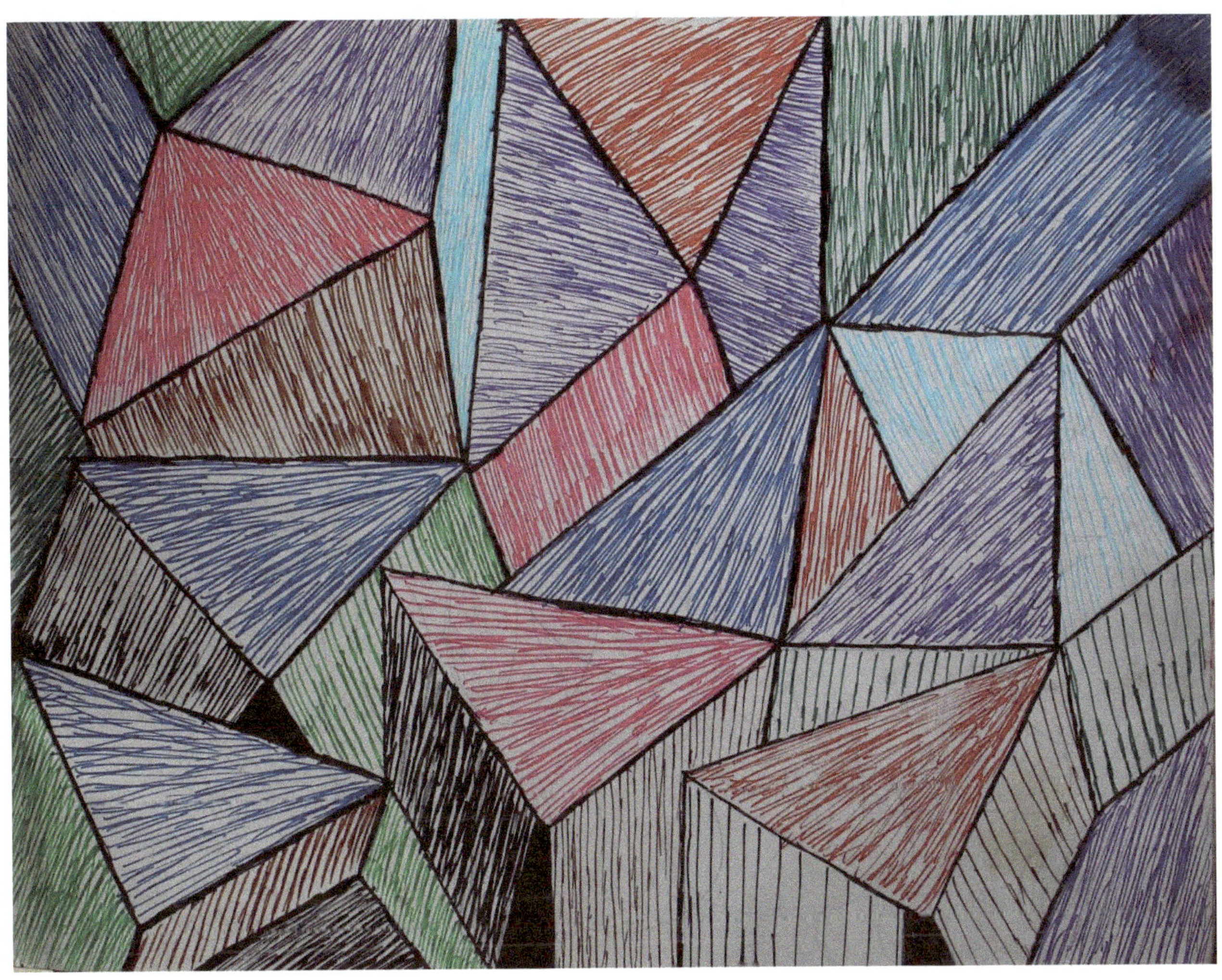

~~Unnamed 22~~
Mediums: felt pen ink on paper
Size: A3
Year: 2021

Lines
        And lines
        And lines
        And lines
Of arching angles
Duneing shapes
Lines
        And lines
        And lines
        And lines
Of ascending land
Reaching out to the skies

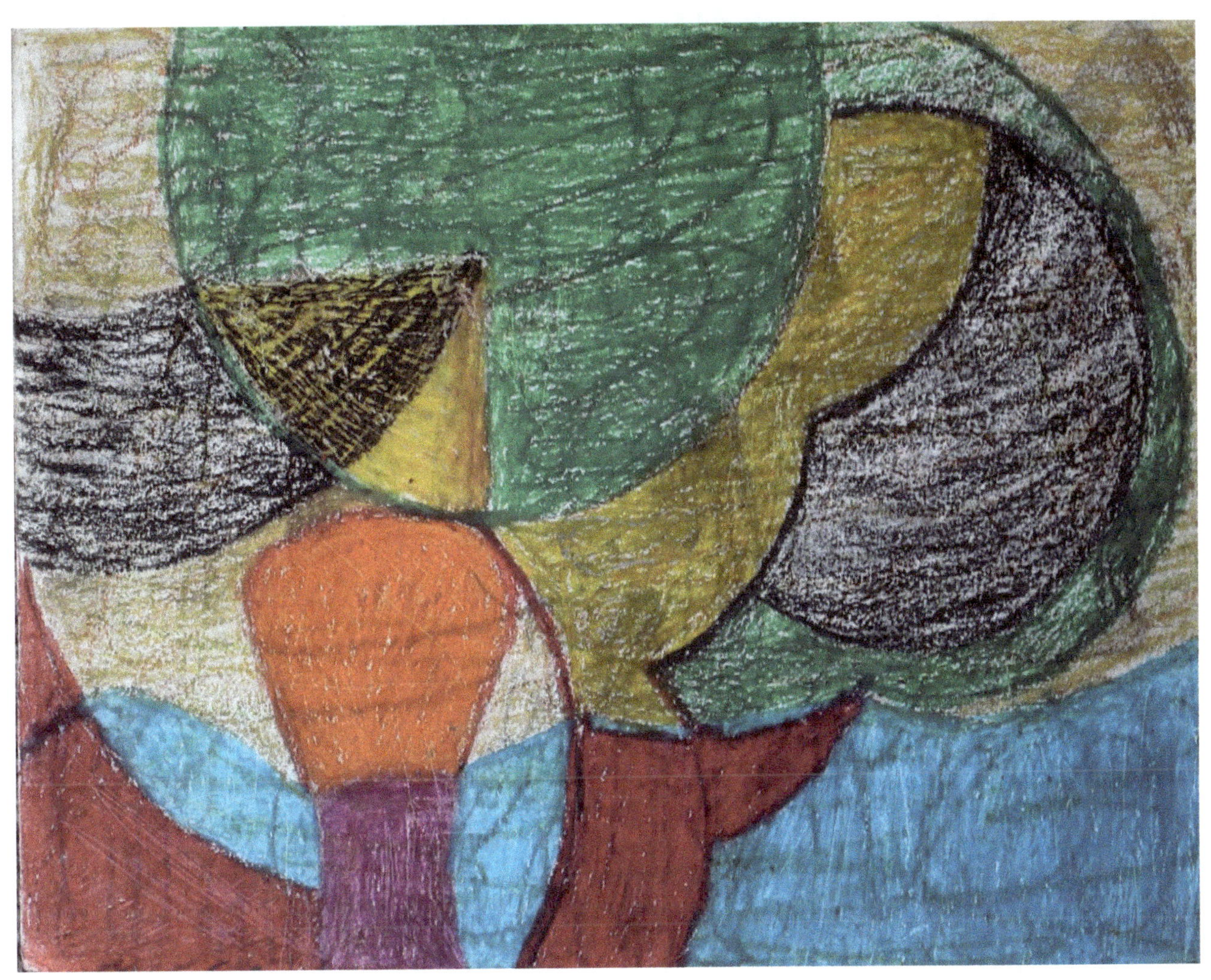

~~Unnamed 23~~
Mediums: oil pastels on paper
Size: A4
Year: 2018

To account
The amount
Around
And around
Circles
abounding
a bounty
of zeroes

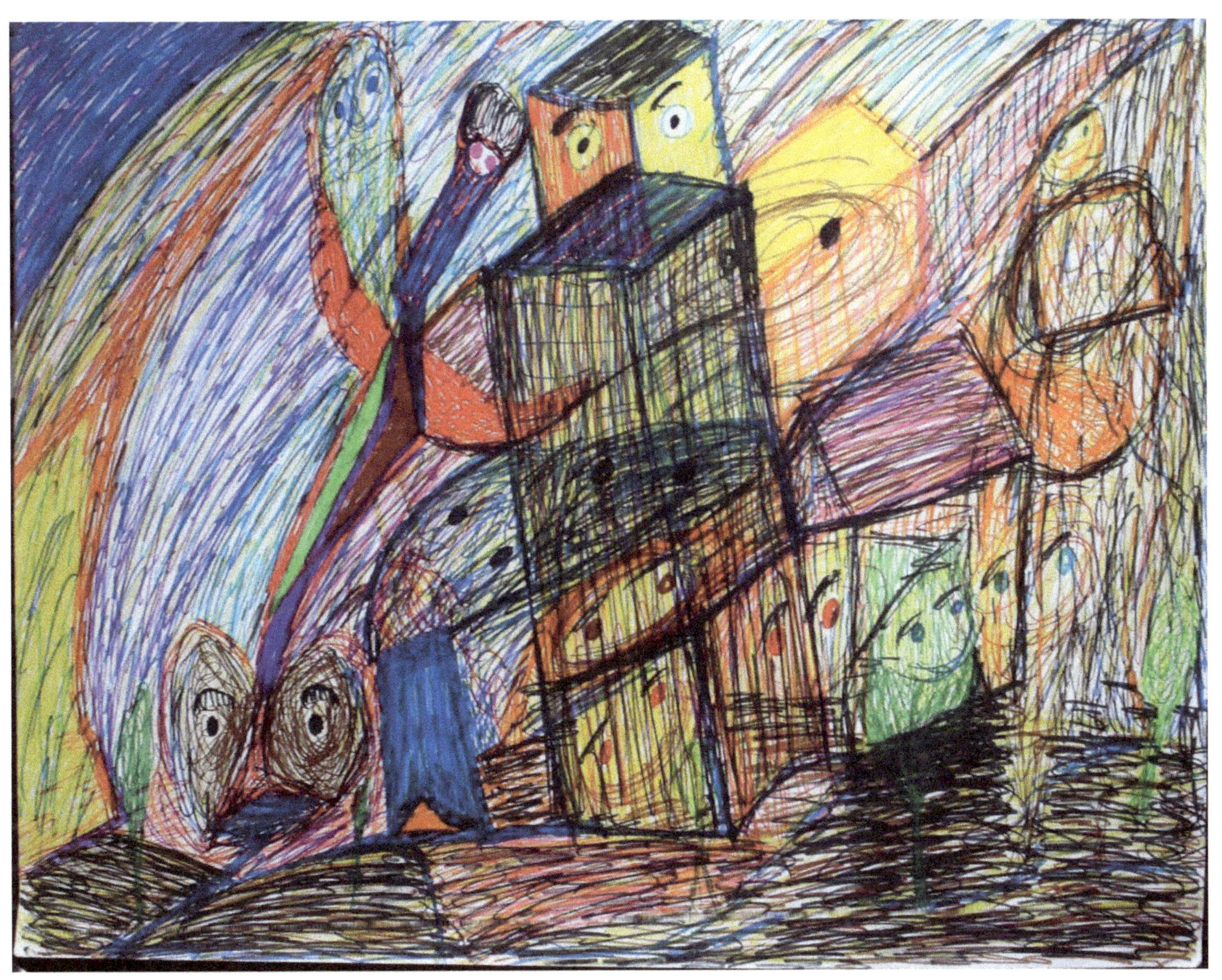

~~Unnamed 24~~
Mediums: felt pen ink and fibre pen ink on paper
Size: A3
Year: 2022

Eyes
Eyes
Eyes
Eyes
Eyes
That see
What they don't see

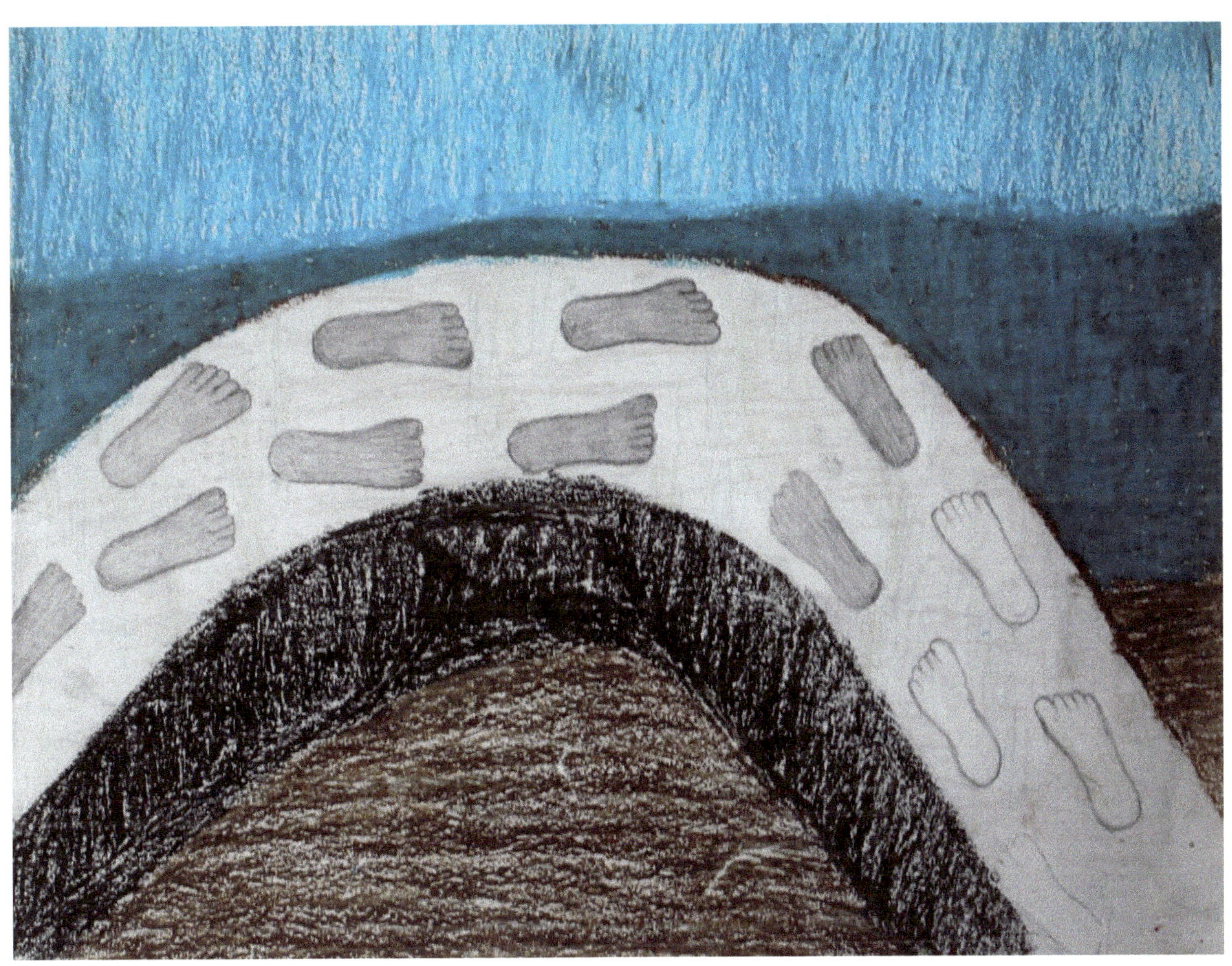

~~Unnamed 25~~
Mediums: graphite and oil pastels on paper
Size: A4
Year: 2018

Path to places
Shadows of footfalls
Adoration to names
And to the feet that
Embellishes this...
Allegiances to surnames,
Bridges that the clock
Connects us to our pasts?

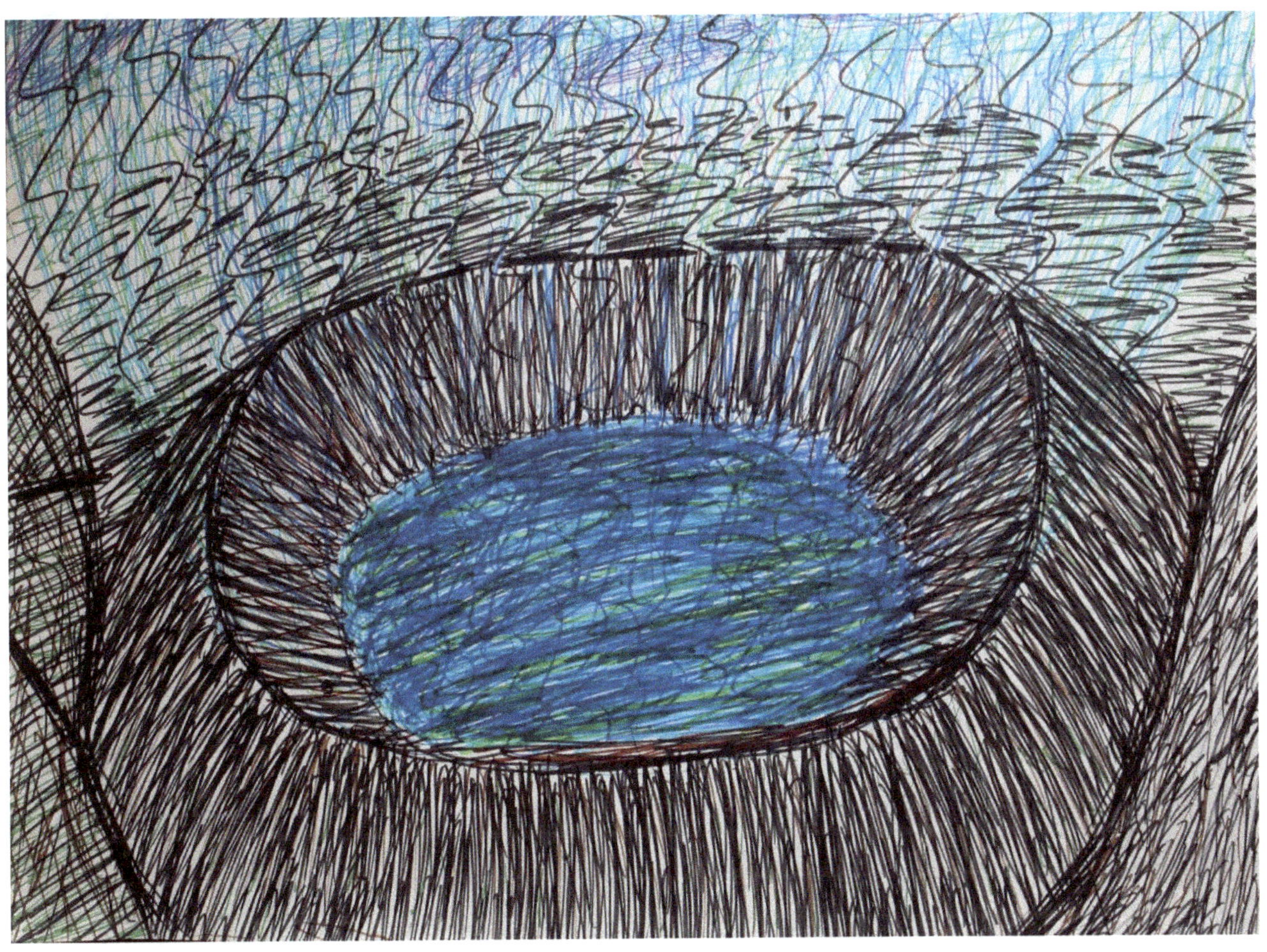

~~Unnamed 26~~

Mediums: fibre ink pen and felt pen ink on paper

Size: A3

Year: 2022

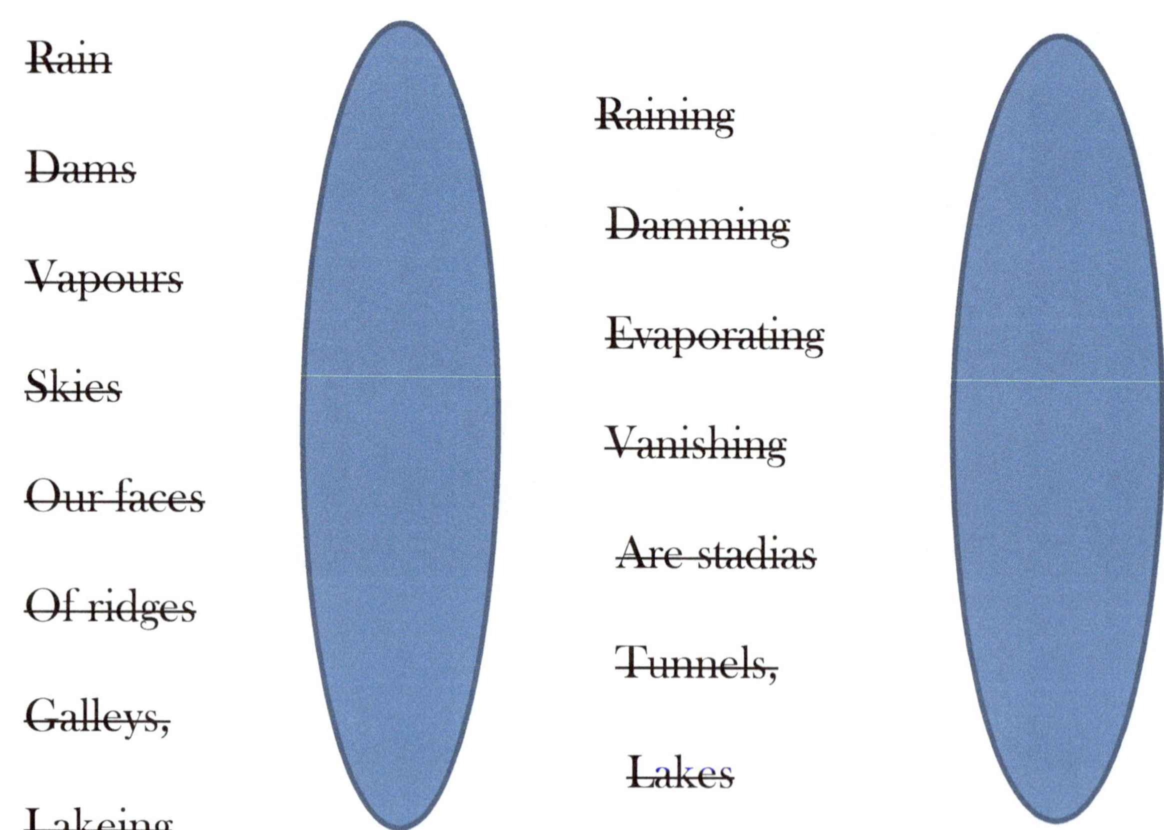

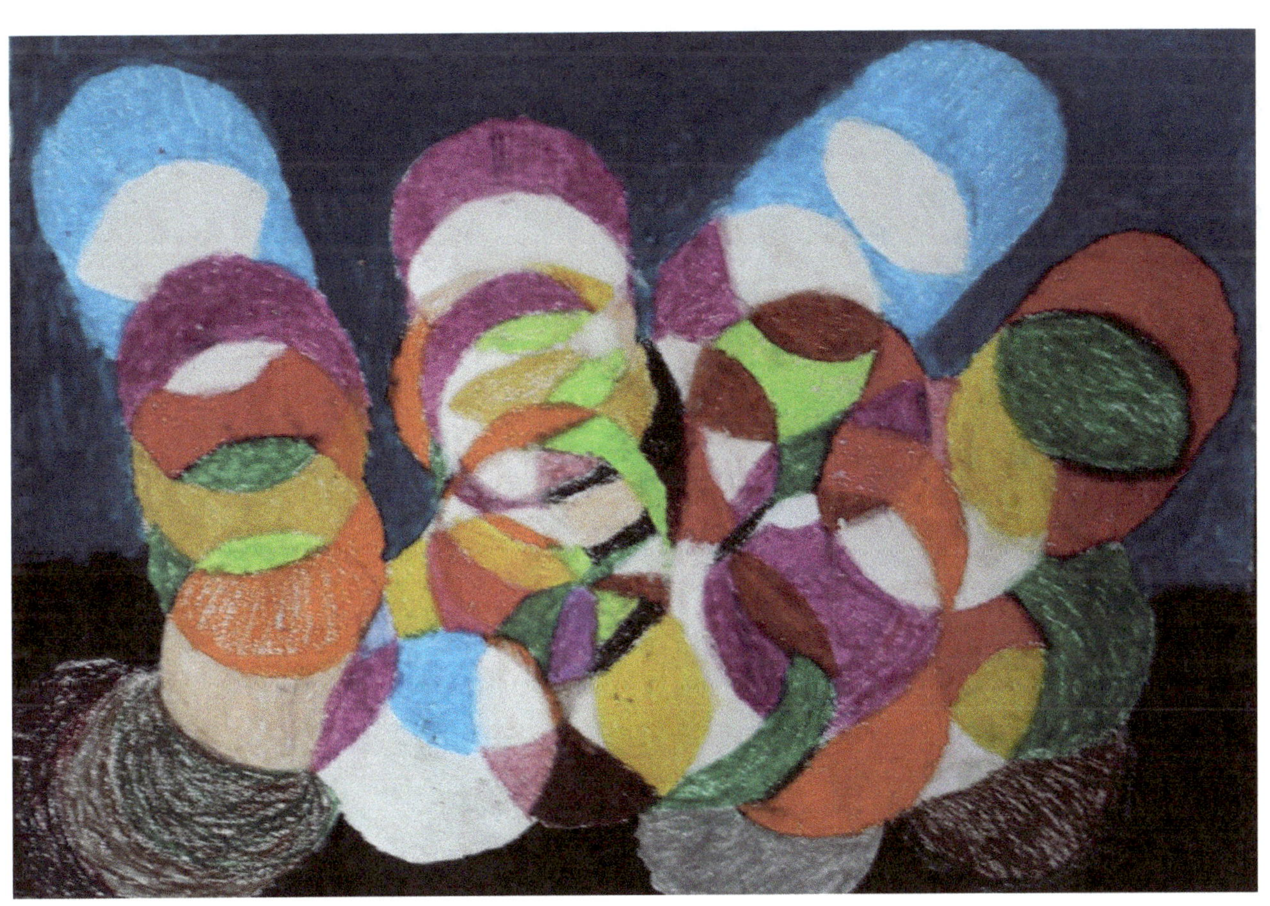

~~Unnamed 27~~
Mediums: oil pastels on paper
Size: A4
Year: 2019

Circles
        Cycling
Circles
        Forward
Circles
        Onward
He, Her, them...
The wind
Is their friend

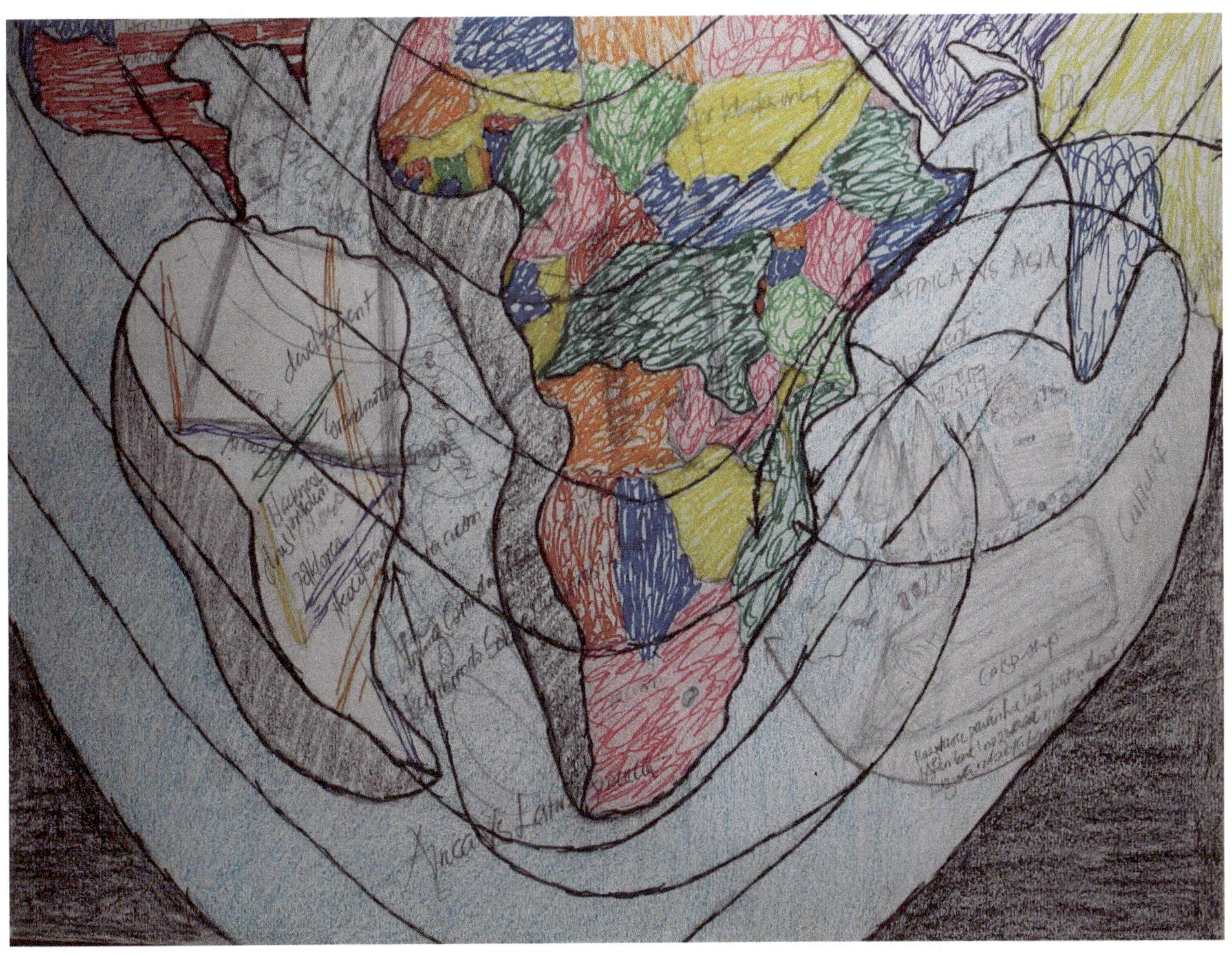

~~Unnamed 28~~
Mediums: graphite, oil pastels, charcoal, fibre ink and ball point ink on paper
Size: A3
Year: 2018

Pangaea
In a language I have forgotten means
distance formed us
in dispersing us

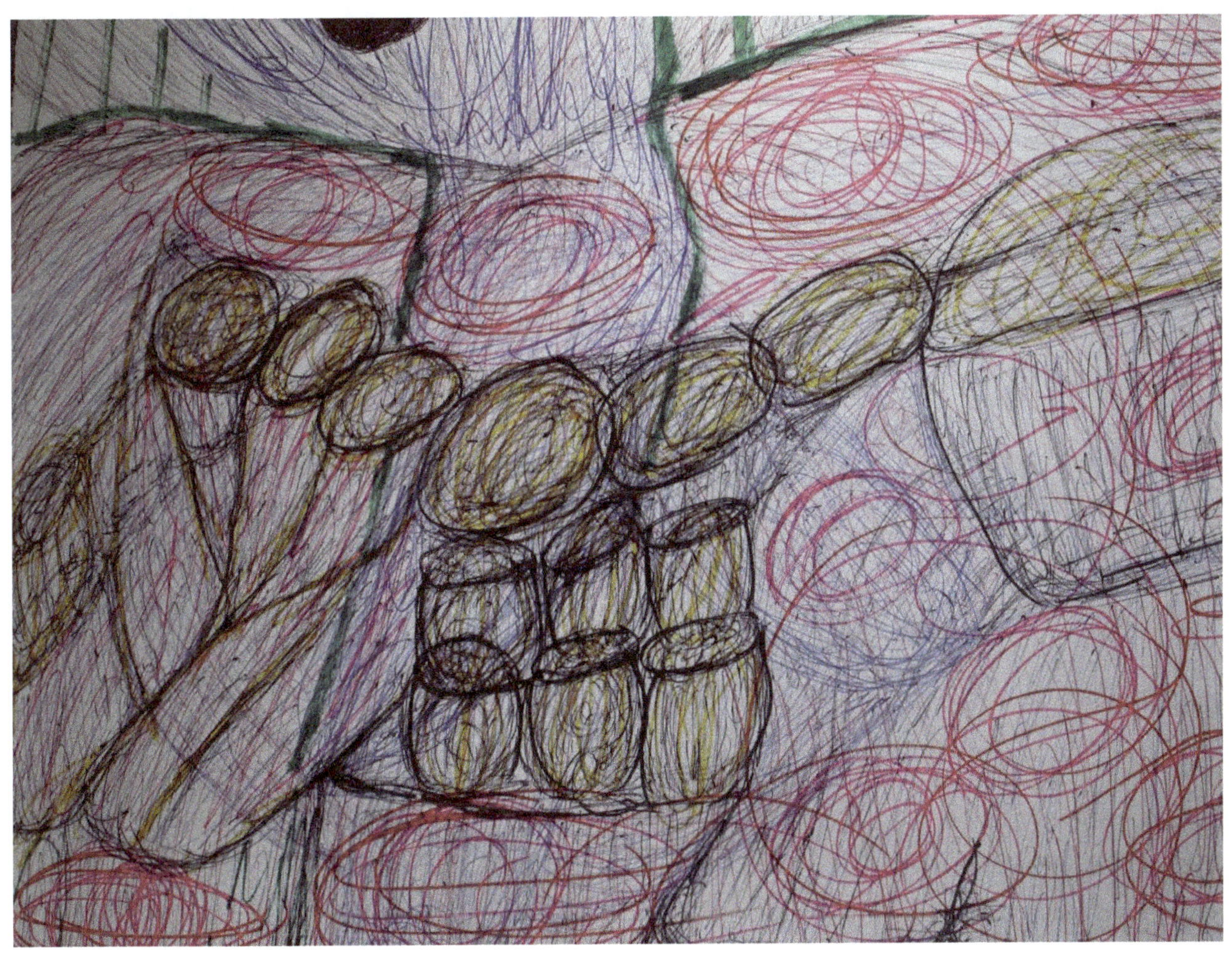

~~Unnamed 29~~
Mediums: graphite, ball point pen ink, fibre pen ink on paper
Size: A3
Year: 2018

~~Balls~~
I didn't say that,
Boulders
Containers
For rolling ~~balls~~
Limbs
Filaments
Connections
And for him, his pen
Always employed by the swirling lines

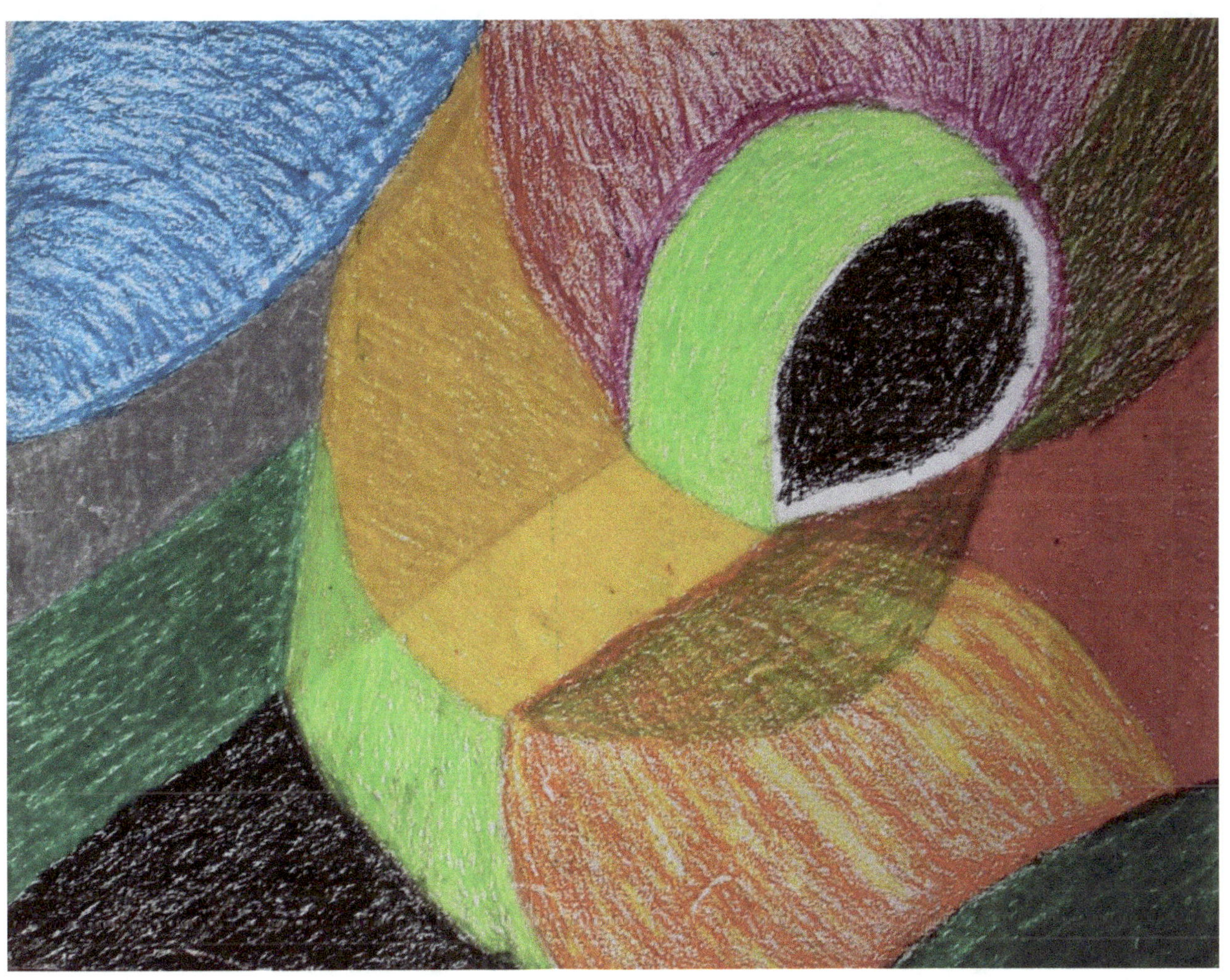

~~Unnamed 30~~
Mediums: oil pastels on paper
Size: A4
Year: 2018

In the calm eye of the storm
Is when we sit down, still down,
Calm, exhausted, conciliatory...
Trying to find safe words to the anger
That has driven us apart
So we coin safe words for hunger
That assuages empty spaces between us
Leaving us skeletal, more angrier than hungry
And we coin safe words to the lies
That with secrecy our spines shamelessly carries
We coin safe words to protect other humans
At the mercies of these winds of our mouths
We coin safe words to future paths
To house us when the storm takes over

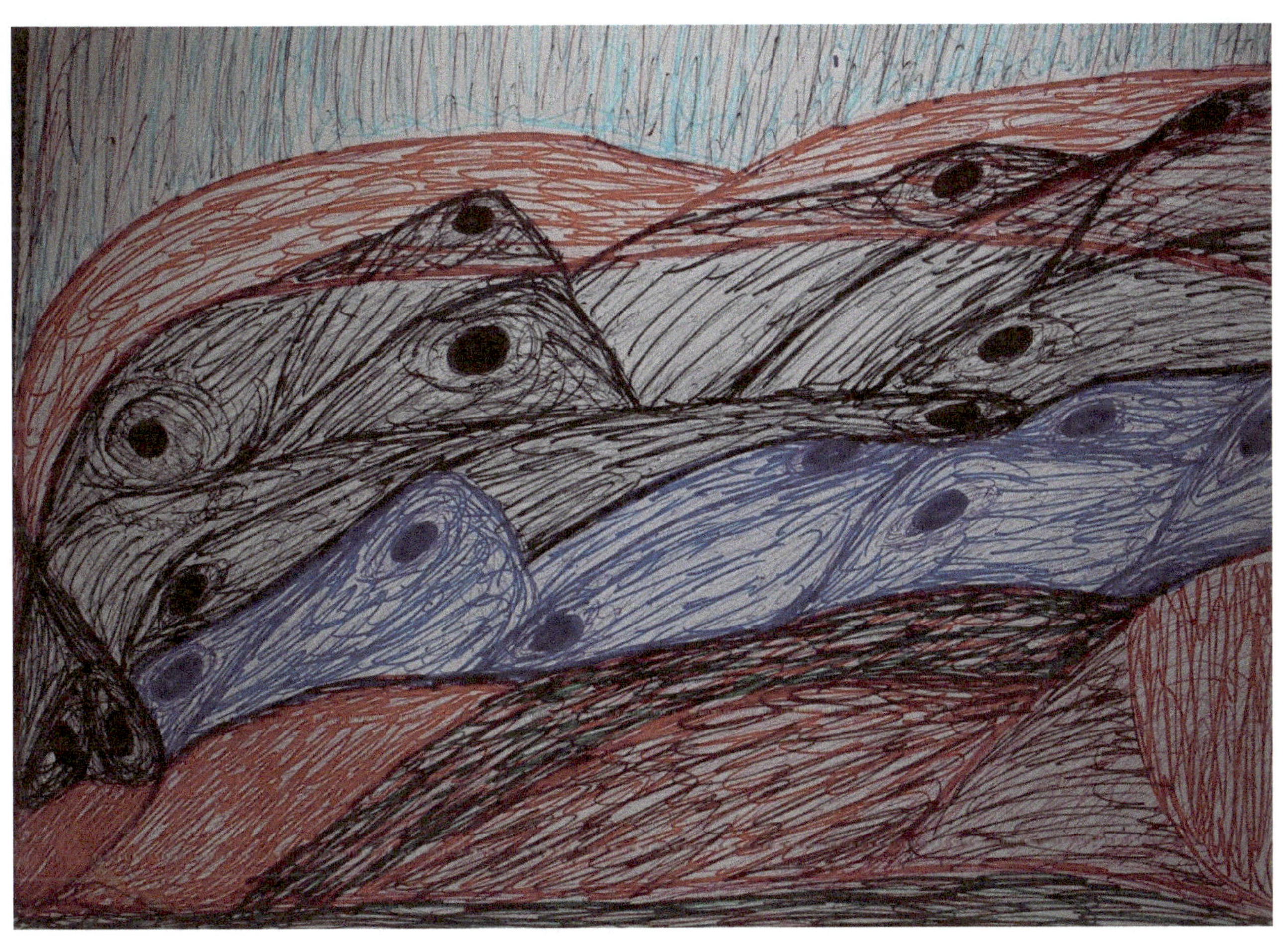

~~Unnamed 31~~
Mediums: ball point ink and fibre ink pen on paper
Size: A3
Year: 2018

Walking on lands
that are mounds,
that are boobies
eyes on boobies....
Sleeping body bags
bodies lying inside
eyes seeing outside

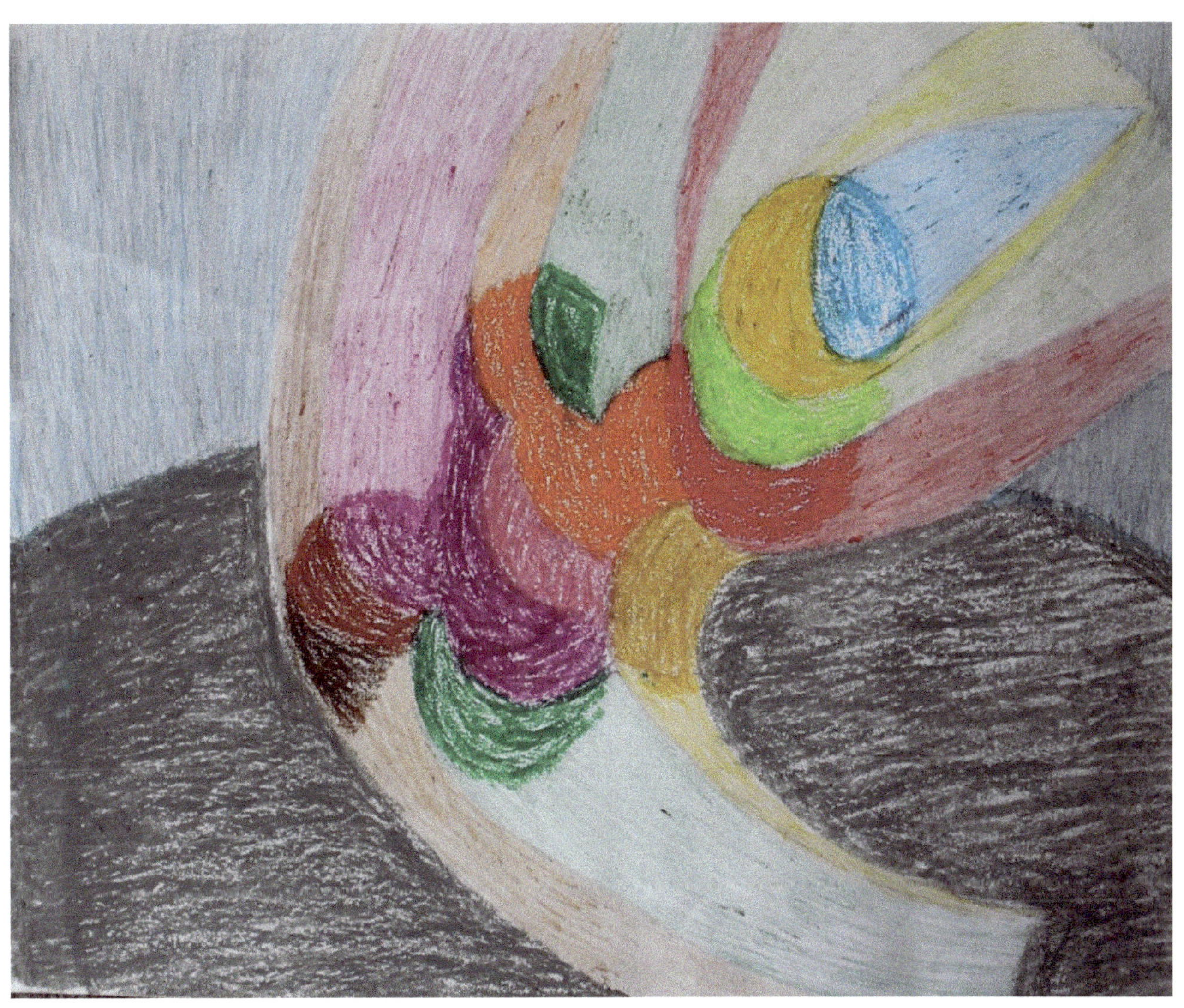

~~Unnamed 32~~
Mediums: graphite, oil pastels, and fibre ink pen on paper
Size: A4
Year: 2019

In the wings of the wind
Ambitions flying high
Into rainbows of happiness
~~In the wings of the wind~~

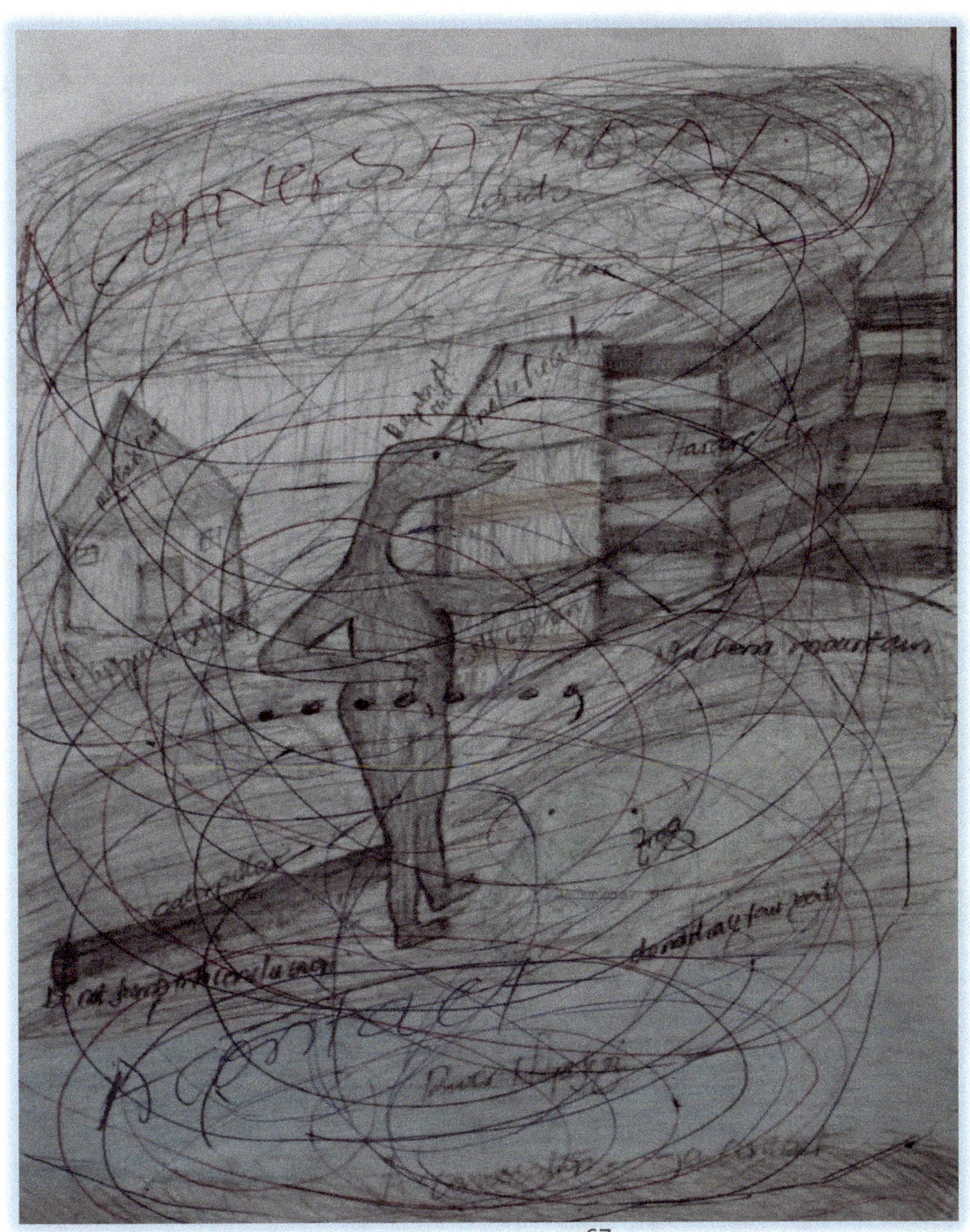
A CONVERSATION

~~Unnamed 33~~
Mediums: graphite, crayons, fibre ink pen and ball point pen ink on paper
Size: A4
Year: 2018

A conversation ~~between tree leaves trickled in~~
~~As it had me stabbing myself~~
....
~~Going back home~~
~~is finding the same trees~~
~~waiting for you~~
or is it a contact,
And then you realise
you had come back
as if you had not come back
and now you don't have to stay
in order for you to leave
and you don't need to leave
in order for you to stay

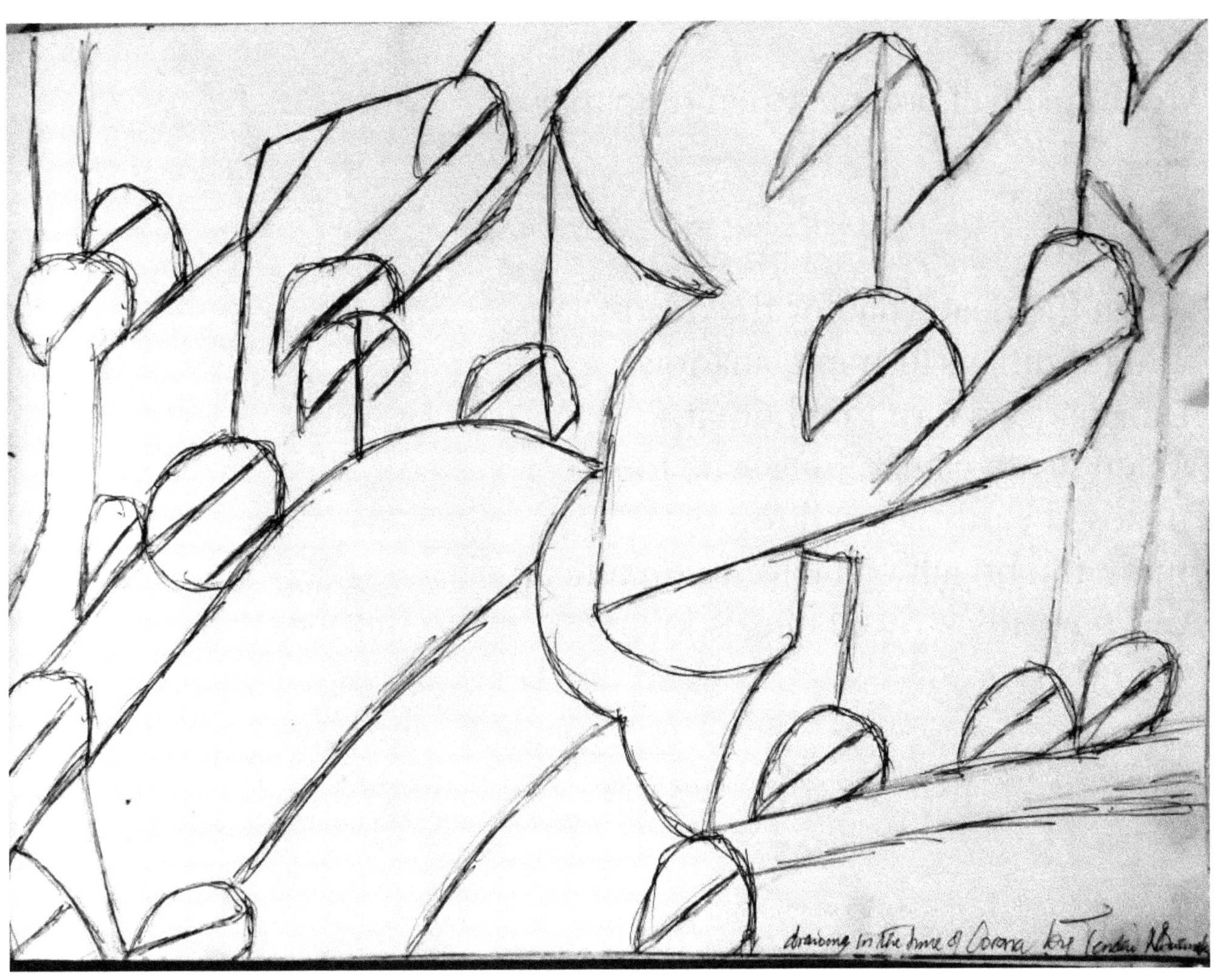
drawing in the time of Corona by Tendai

~~Unnamed 34~~
Mediums: ball point ink pen on paper
Size: A4
Year: 2020

When the dead vote for the dead
When humans turn into shadows
And shadows turn into humans
When death can no longer be found
In closed earths, closed tombs
But in the breath you have to breathe
And our only way of being is killing

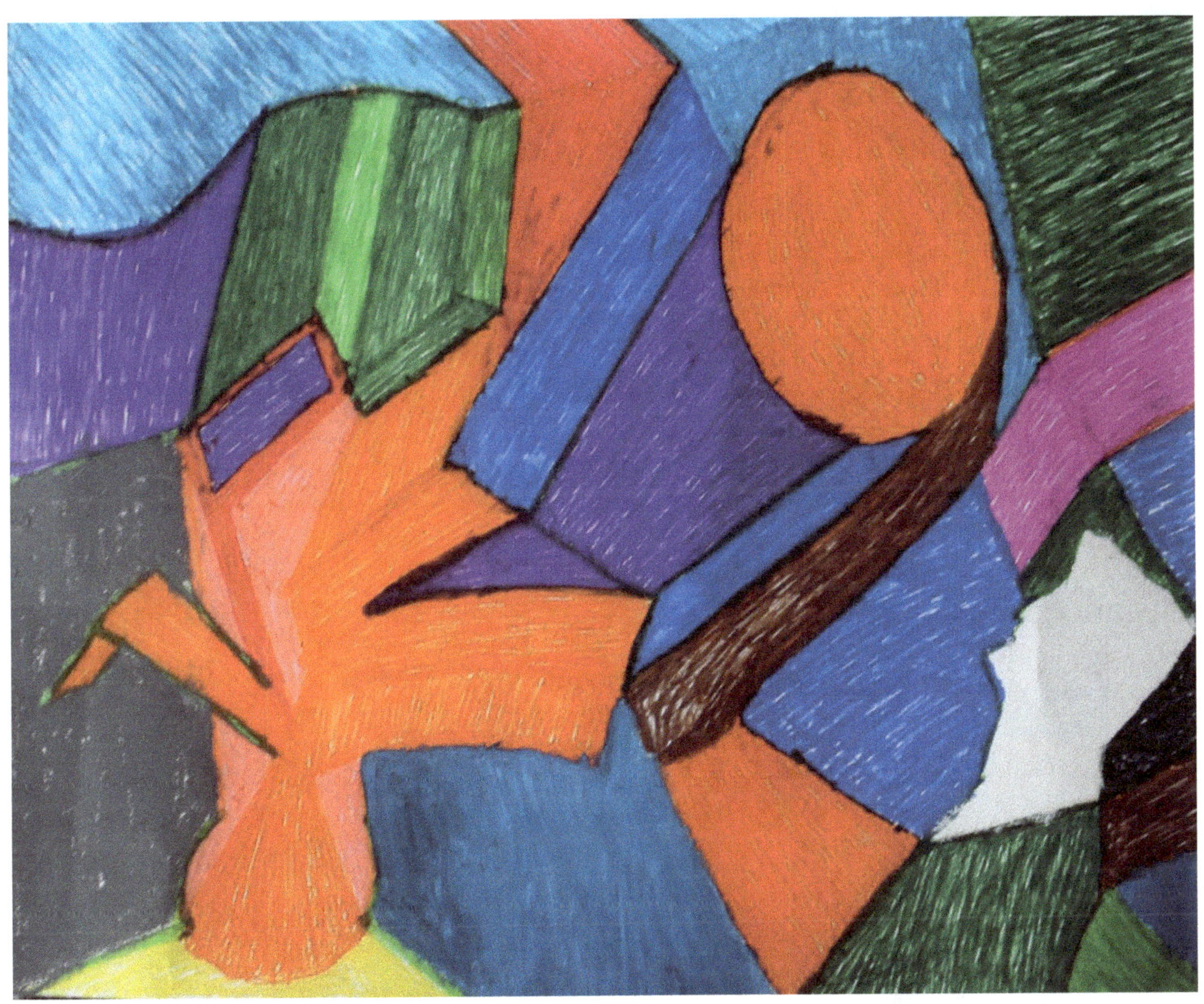

~~Unnamed 35~~
Mediums: oil pastels, fibre ink pen and felt pen ink on paper
Size: A4
Year: 2020

His face like the sun
His face like the world
His face like the centre of the universe
Which is anywhere you stand now
You are in there, at the centre
Distanced from yourself
You are only human
You are at odds with yourself
You can only unchanged yourself

~~His face like~~
~~His face anywhere~~
~~He is you~~
~~You are only from human~~
~~You at odds unchanged~~
~~You are only yourself~~
~~You can like the world~~
~~You can like the centre of now~~
~~You stand the centre yourself~~

IN THIS SEA

I WOULD SWIM IN THE CUP OF THIS MOON
AN ABIENT SEA IMAGING AROUND ME
TOLL SIGHS CLINGING TO MY DARKLING SKIN
THE WHITE WIND NEIGHING ABOVE THIS SEA
RETURNING TO HAUNT ME AGAIN AND AGAIN
THE LUMINOUS FLAMES OF MY DISTANT PAST
NOW THEY NEVER LEAVE ME ALONE
I LISTENED TO THE SOOTHING VOICE WITHIN THEM
THE BELL OF A WONDERING COW IN WINTER
LIKE THE MOURNING TOLL OF A FARROWING PLOUGH

I AM THE SOUND AND ONLY SOUL IN THIS SEA

#Symphony of my Soul.

I dluow mmiws ni eht puc fo siht noom
dna tneiba aes gnigami dnuora em
llot shgis gnignilc ot ym gnikrad niks
eht etihw dniw gnihgien evoba siht aes
gninruter ot tnuah em niaga dna niaga
eht suonimul semalf fo ym tnatsid tsap
won yeht reven evael em enola
I denetsil ot eht gnihtoos eciov nihtiw meht
eht lleb fo a gnirednow woc ni retniw
ekil eht gninruom llot fo a gniworraf hguolp

~~Unnamed 36~~
Mediums: ball point pen ink and fibre ink pen on paper
Size: A4
Year: 2021

~~*"I would swim in the cup of this moon*~~
~~*An ambient sea imaging around me*~~
~~*Toll sighs clinging to my darkling skin*~~
~~*The white wind neighing above this sea*~~
~~*Returning to haunt me again and again*~~
~~*The luminous flames of my distant past*~~
~~*No, they never leave me alone..."*~~

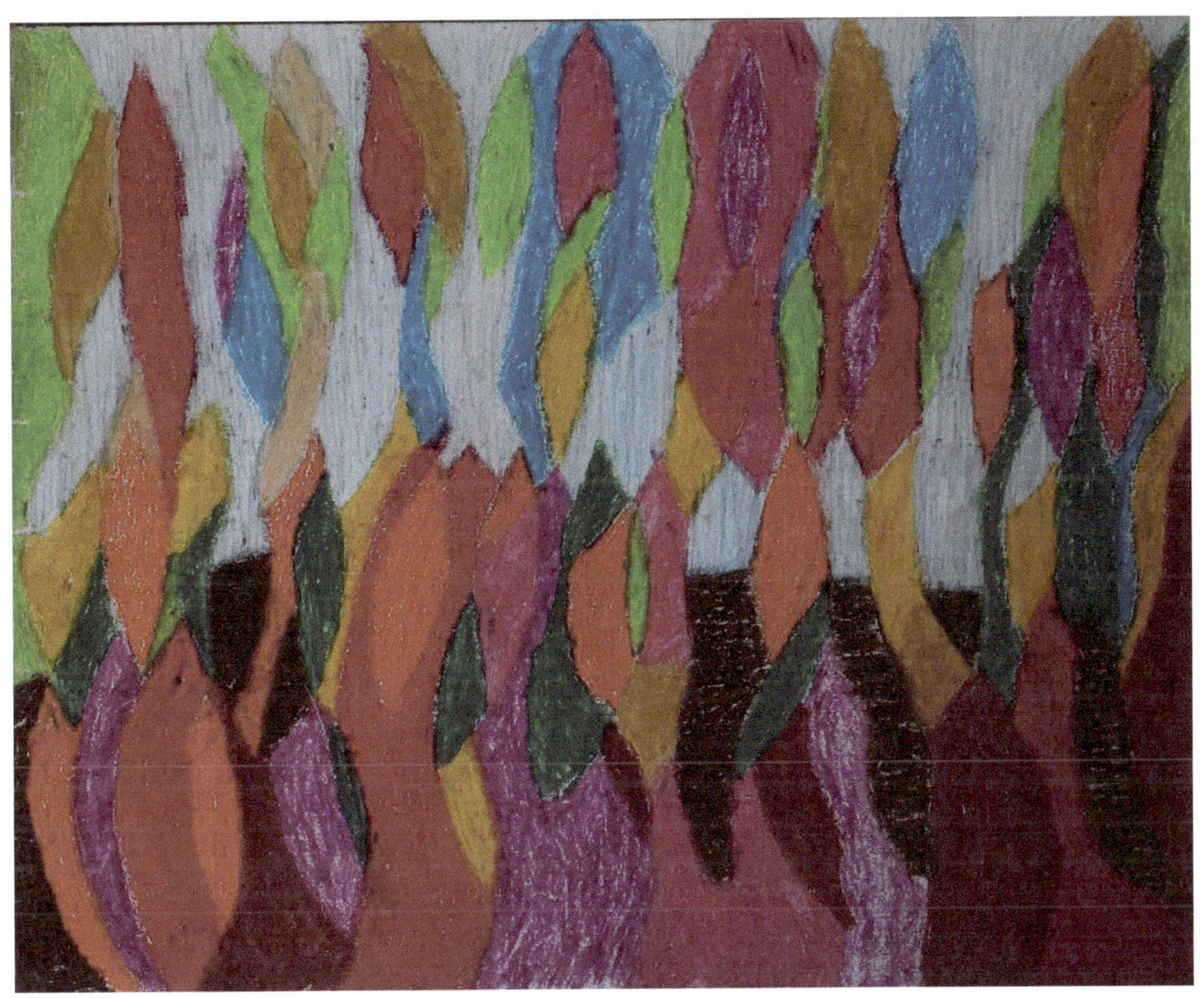

~~Unnamed 37~~
Mediums: oil pastels on paper
Size: A4
Year: 2020

The alphabets of humanity singing in the sun
Moaning human harmonies
Watching mothers who weren't ours
Waiting for children that weren't theirs
Laughter becoming painful needles
Where pain has no tears
These are the woman who will be waiting for you

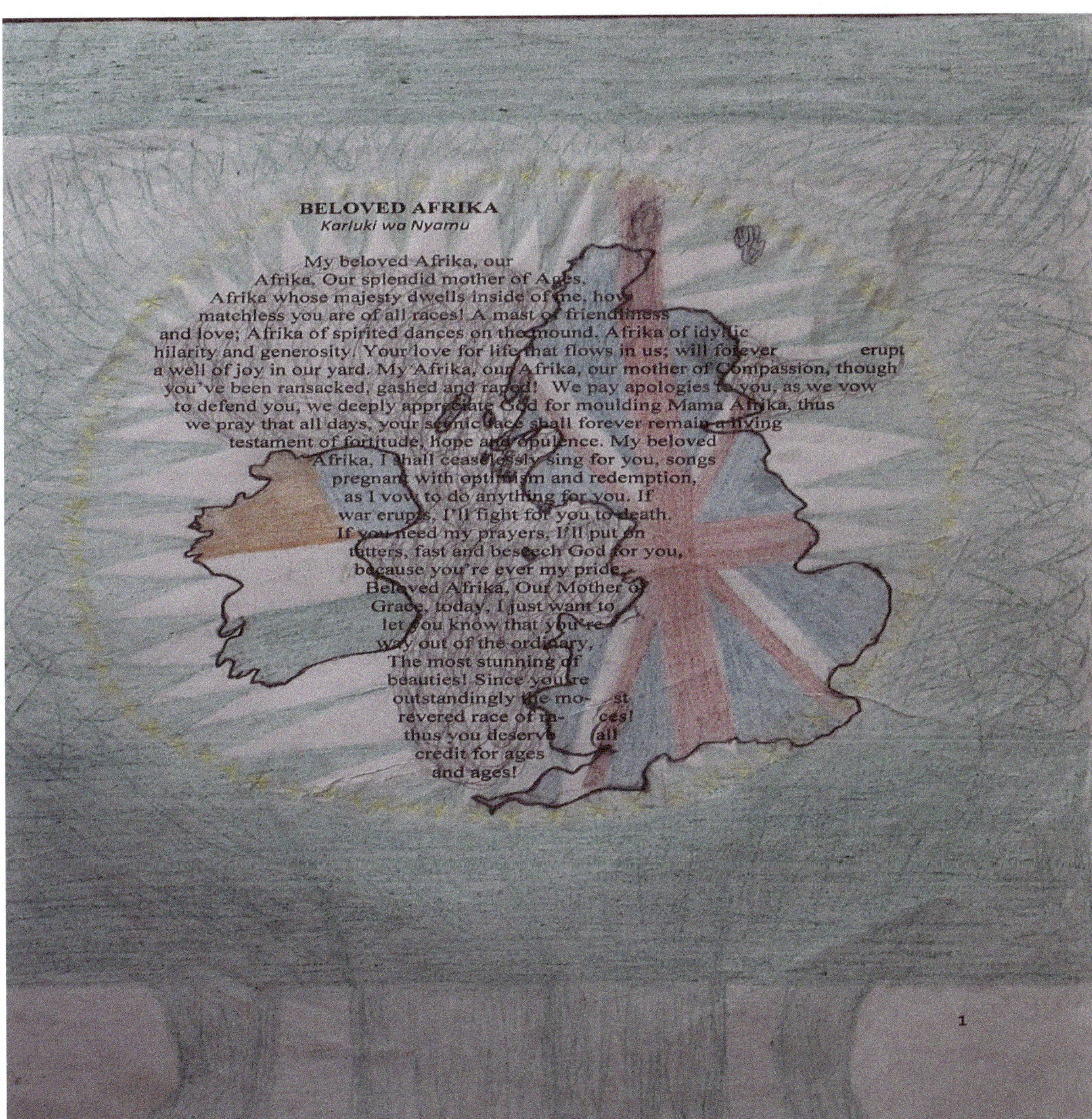
BELOVED AFRIKA
Kariuki wa Nyamu
My beloved Afrika, our
Afrika. Our splendid mother of Ages,
Afrika whose majesty dwells inside of me, how
matchless you are of all races! A mast of friendliness
and love; Afrika of spirited dances on the mound. Afrika of idyllic
hilarity and generosity. Your love for life that flows in us; will forever erupt
a well of joy in our yard. My Afrika, our Afrika, our mother of Compassion, though
you've been ransacked, gashed and raped! We pay apologies to you, as we vow
to defend you, we deeply appreciate God for moulding Mama Afrika, thus
we pray that all days, your scenic face shall forever remain a living
testament of fortitude, hope and opulence. My beloved
Afrika, I shall ceaselessly sing for you, songs
pregnant with optimism and redemption,
as I vow to do anything for you. If
war erupts, I'll fight for you to death.
If you need my prayers, I'll put on
tatters, fast and beseech God for you,
because you're ever my pride.
Beloved Afrika, Our Mother of
Grace, today, I just want to
let you know that you're
way out of the ordinary,
The most stunning of
beauties! Since you're
outstandingly the mo- st
revered race of ra- ces!
thus you deserve all
credit for ages
and ages!
1

~~Unnamed 38~~
Mediums: felt pen ink and printed poem on paper
Size: A4
Year: 2018

~~Write what you want to write~~

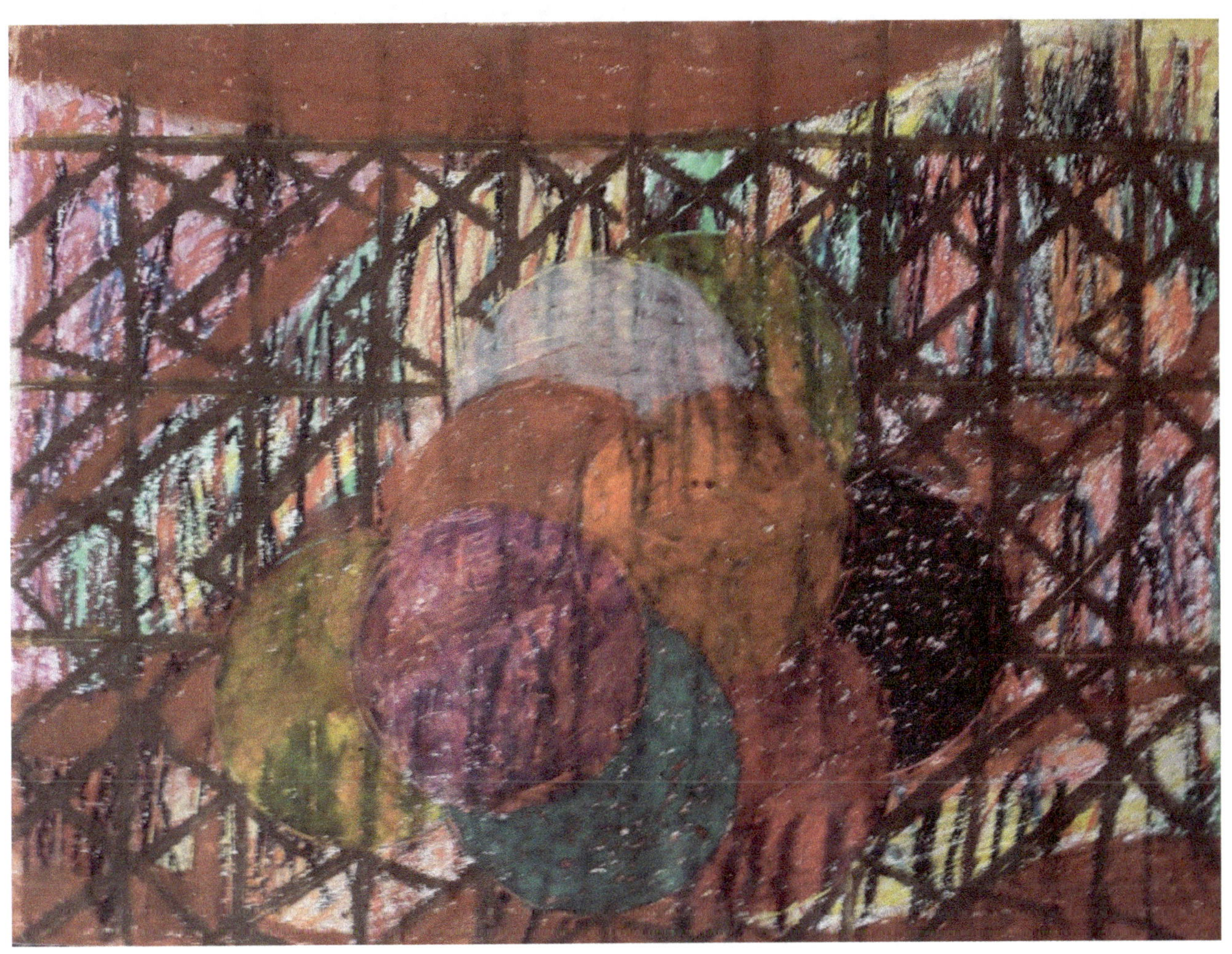

~~Unnamed 39~~
Mediums: oil pastels on paper
Size: A4
Year: 2020

Indelible memories are red tape
Evoking the desire of breaking
Out of its bars and chains

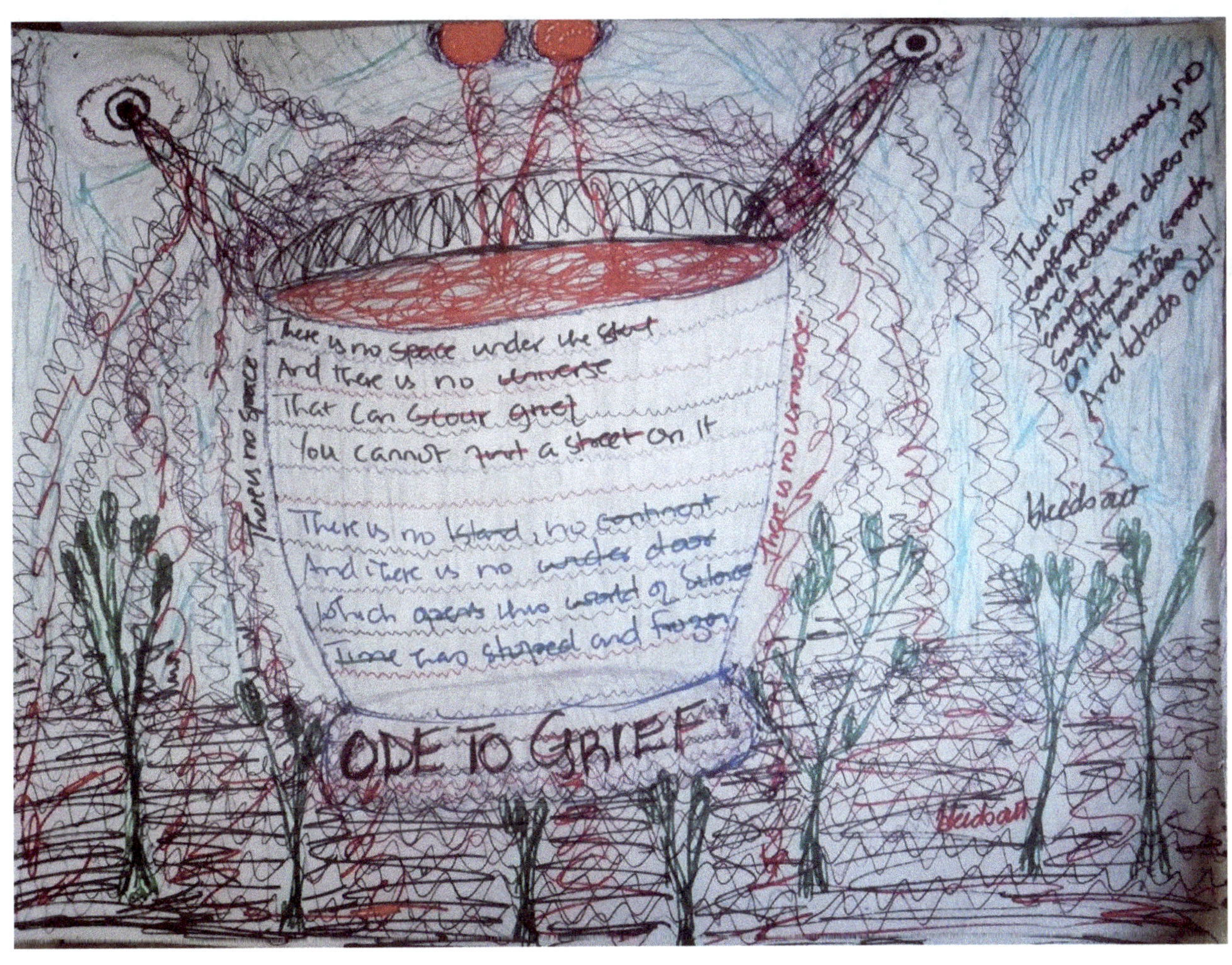
There is no space under the
And there is no universe
That can
You cannot
There is no island, no
And there is no
ODE TO GRIEF
There is no space
There is no universe
There is no
And the ocean does not
And bleeds out!
bleeds out

~~Unnamed 40~~

Mediums: fibre ink pen, ball point pen ink and felt pen ink on paper

Size: A3

Year: 2021

~~There is no space under the sky~~
~~And they is no universe~~
~~That can scour grief~~
~~There is no tremor, nor earthquake~~
~~And the ocean does not empty~~
~~And bleeds the sands on its beaches~~

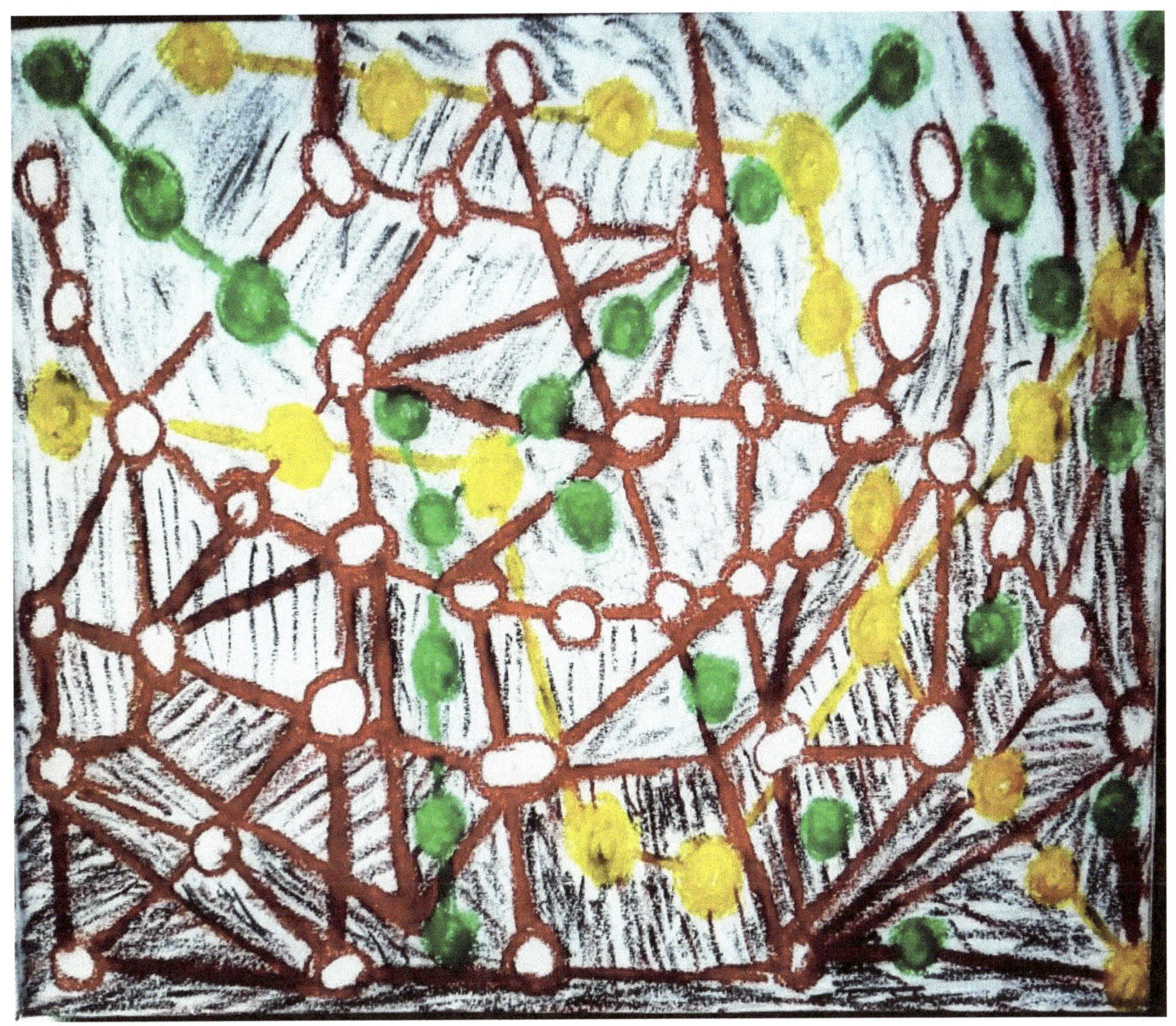

~~Unnamed 41~~
Mediums: oil pastels on paper
Size: A4
Year: 2020

Could this be the birth of
Polka Doltish dots
When form follows flow
Or they are stars
like locomotives on incline

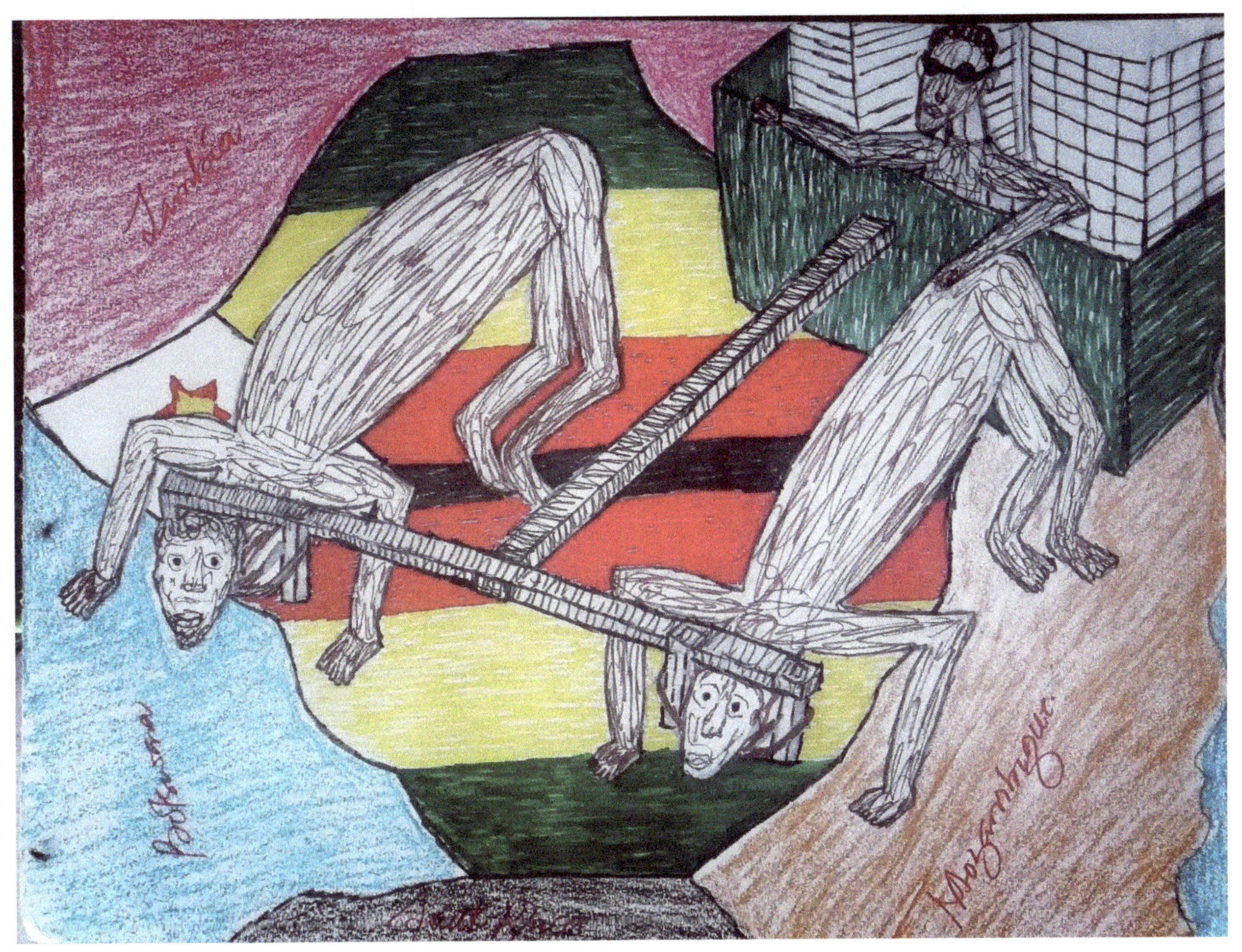
Zambia
Botswana
Mozambique

~~Unnamed 42~~
Mediums: crayons, oil pastels, felt pen ink, ball point pen ink, fibre ink pen on paper
Size: A3
Year: 2018

The more we pull the ox-cart
The more the yoke wields
It's deadening weight on our necks
Is the more we walk
the country of our births
The more it becomes less ours

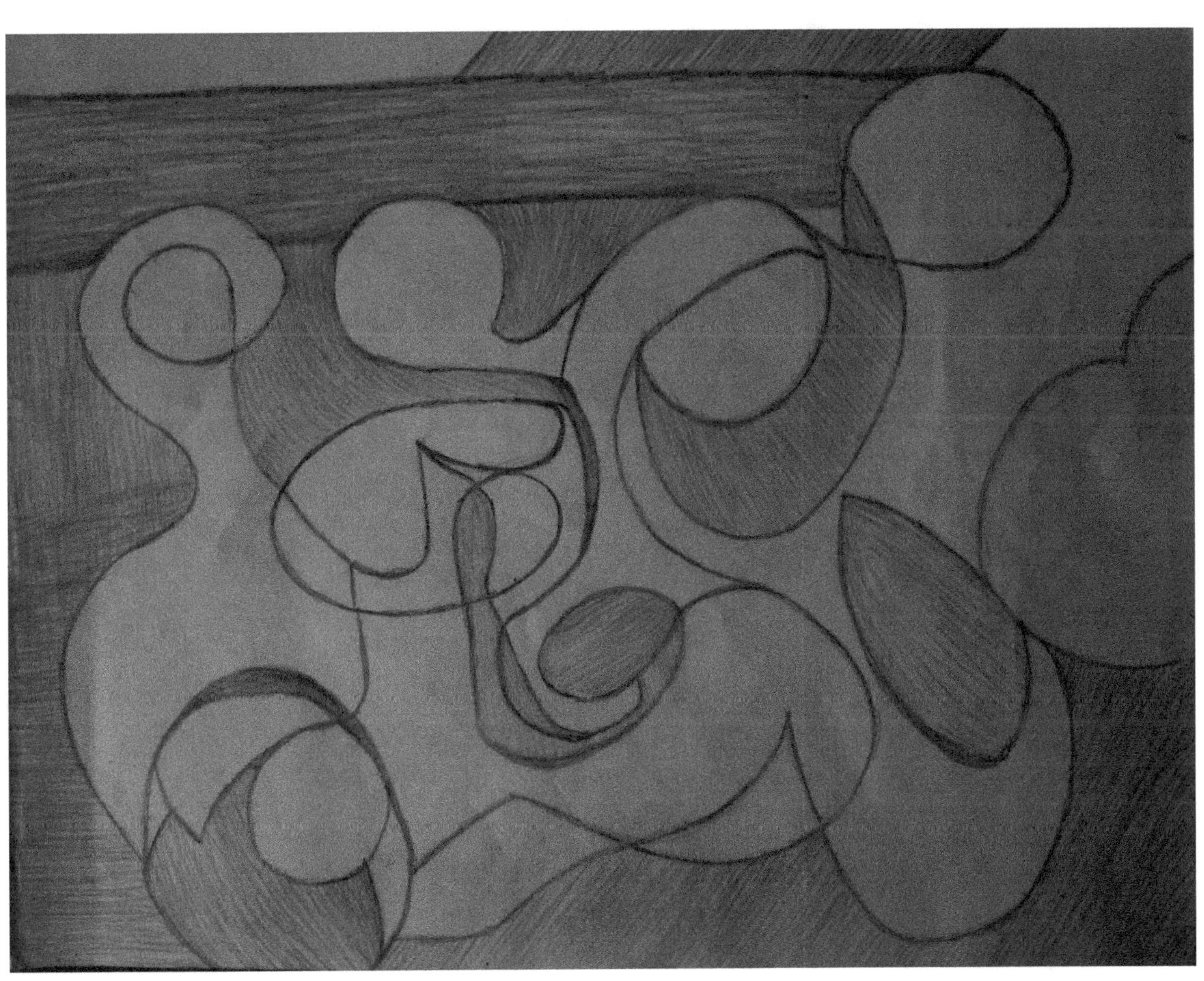

~~Unnamed 43~~
Mediums: graphite on paper
Size: A2
Year: 2021

Earth is mother,
The sky is father
And women hold half of the sky

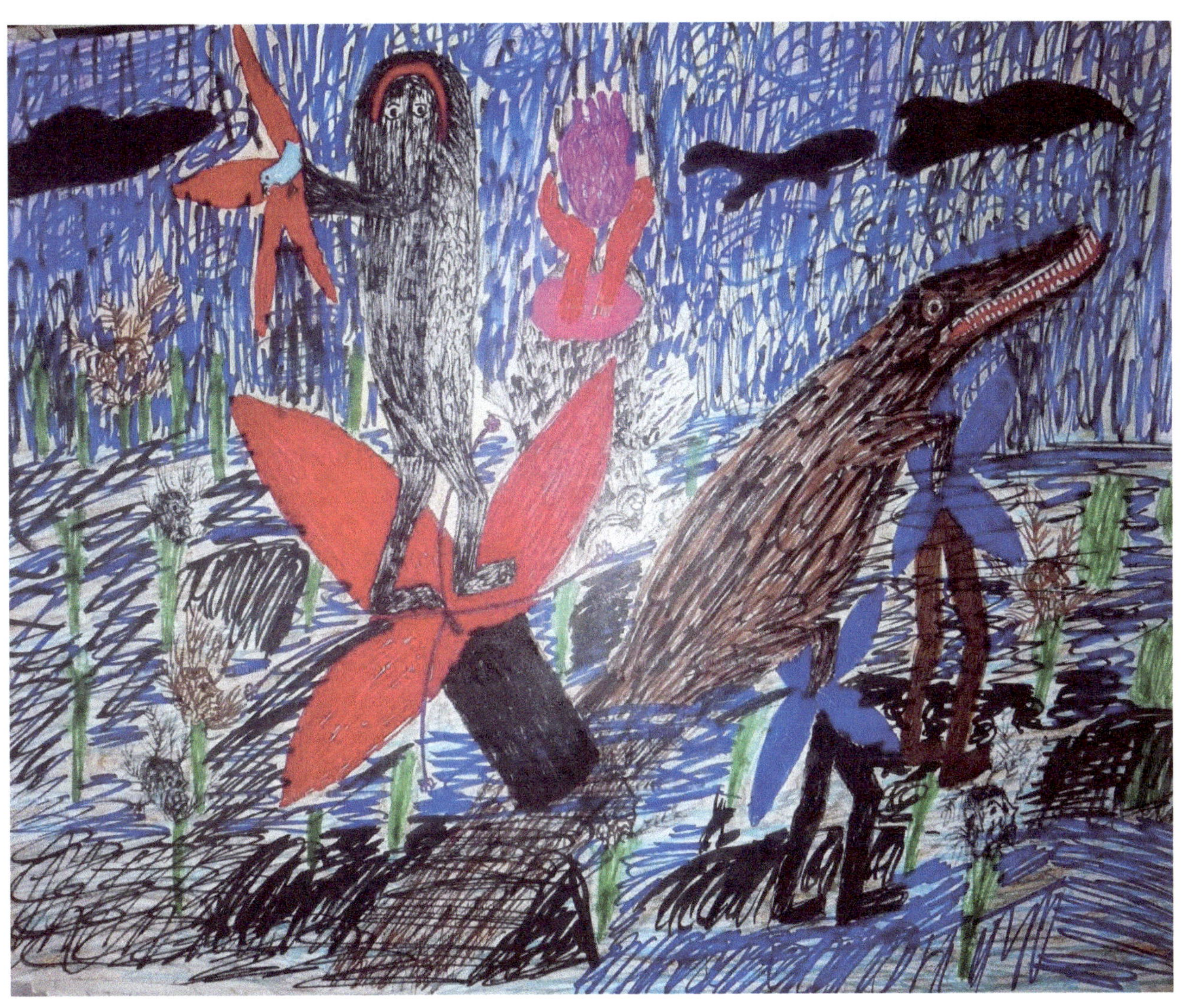

~~Unnamed 44~~
Mediums: markers, felt pen ink, fibre ink pen and oil pastels on paper
Size: A3
Year: 2022

She had read somewhere that naming a plant was as important as naming a person, and that if you select the right name, the plant might live to be hundreds of years old, some a thousand year old.

And that's why he would visit the hulking baobabs

And she had also read from somewhere that someday we might need to create a Will for the plants we kept as pets, telling those we left behind who will inherit the plants when we are gone.

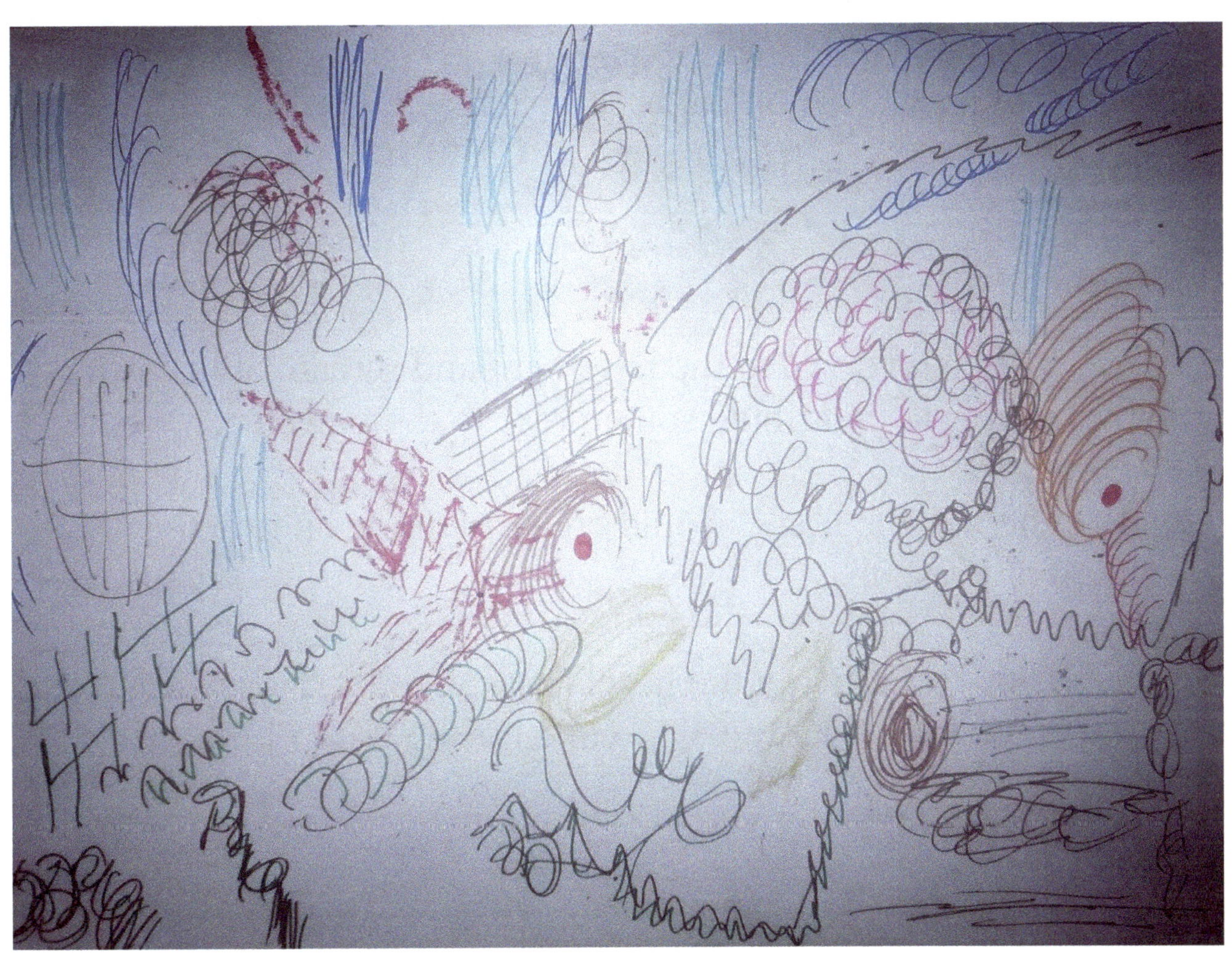

~~Unnamed 45~~
Mediums: fibre ink pen on paper
Size: A3
Year: 2022

He would often go down to the basement and scream at his own shadows simply to contribute some noise to the universe.

He liked the way the noises would create whirling lines in the basement of his soul

Some days he would scout the hazel horizon as the fat sun argued with the encroaching darkness, looking for the wails of the contracting hour

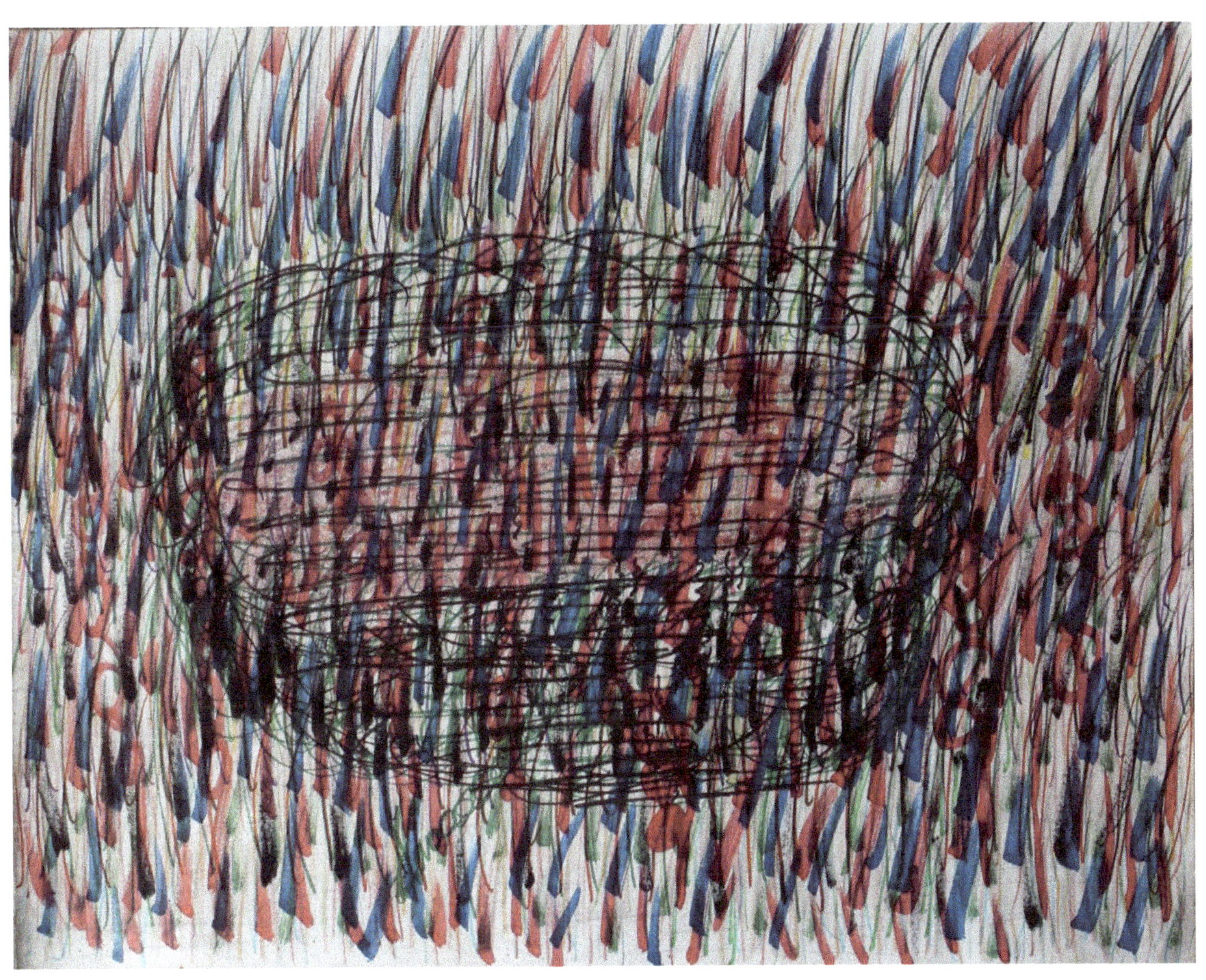

~~Unnamed 46~~
Mediums: fibre ink pen and markers on paper
Size: A4
Year: 2021

Fire’s relationship with fire is
The body’s relationship with body
The body’s thermal mapping
It burns what doesn’t burn
And do not burn what burns

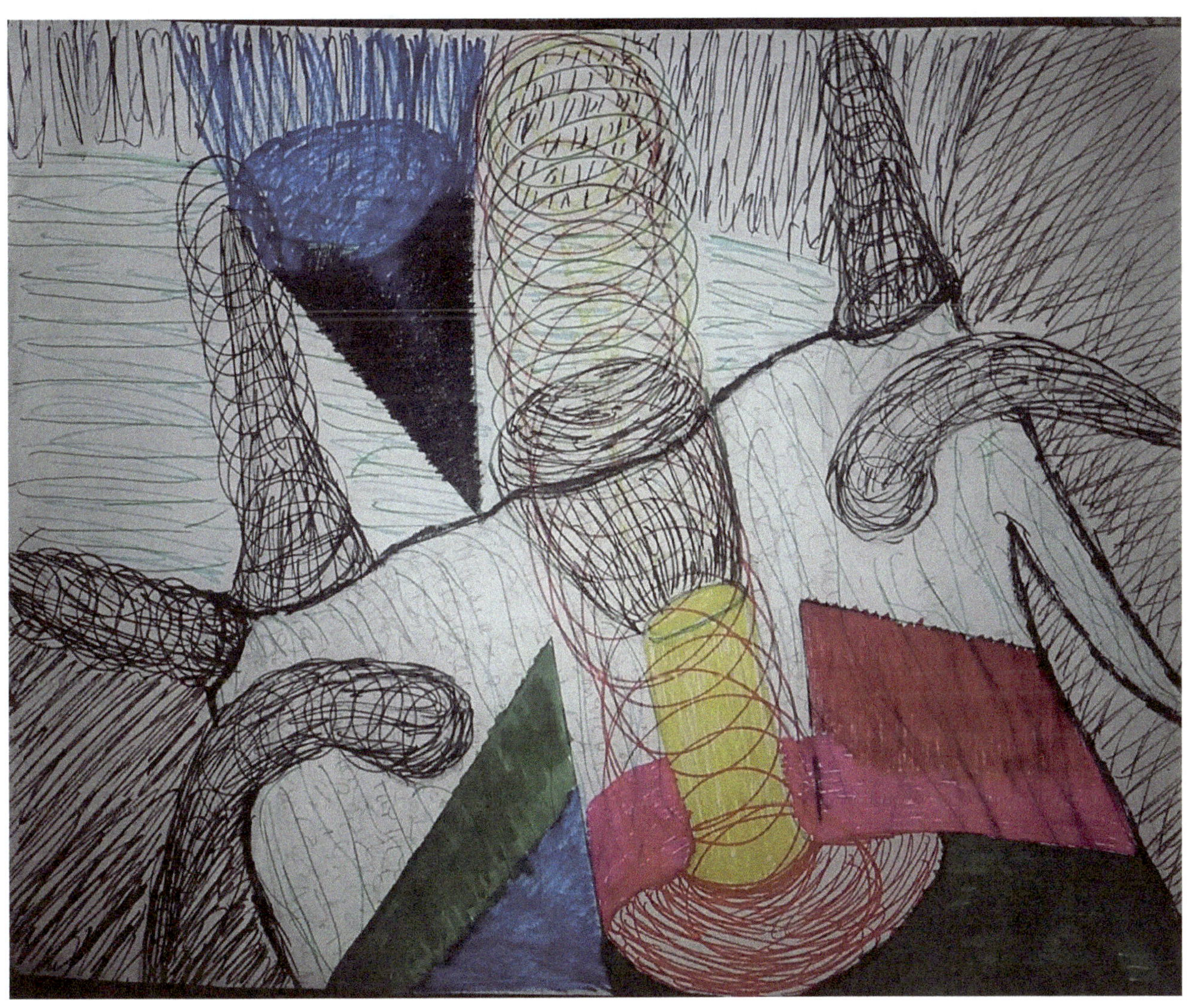

~~Unnamed 47~~
Mediums: markers, fibre ink pen, felt pen ink and ball point pen ink on paper
Size: A3
Year: 2021

You will not know me
You will not meet me
I don't look like one of you

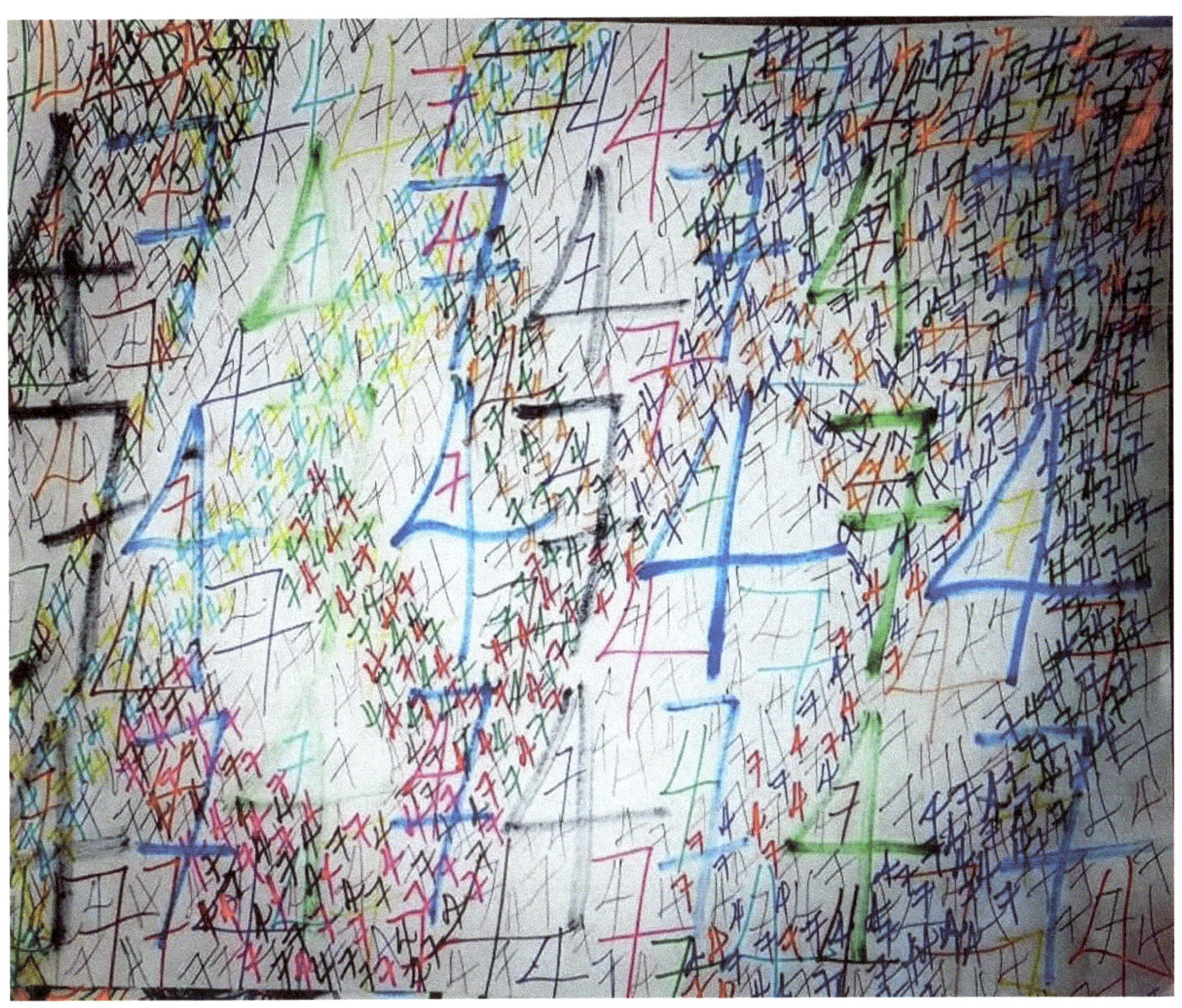

Unnamed 48
Mediums: fibre ink pen and markers on paper
Size: A3
Year: 2021

~~747~~
7777777777777777777777777
~~47~~
4444444444444444444444444
~~7~~
The music of 7 and 4

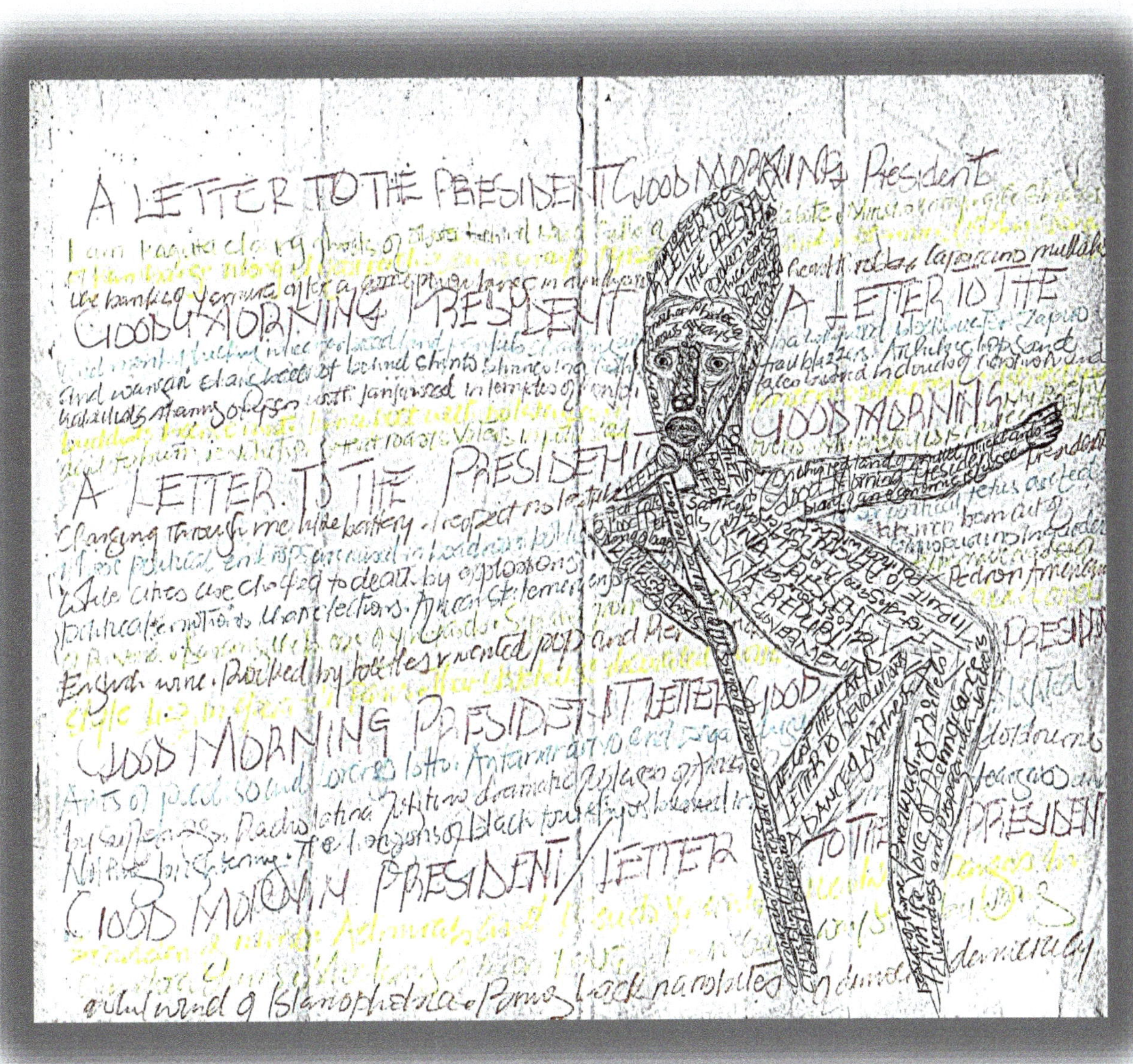
A LETTER TO THE PRESIDENT
GOOD MORNING President
GOOD MORNING PRESIDENT
A LETTER TO THE
GOOD MORNING
A LETTER TO THE PRESIDENT
GOOD MORNING PRESIDENT
GOOD MORNING PRESIDENT / LETTER
PRESIDENT

~~Unnamed 49~~
Mediums: fibre ink pen on paper
Size: A4
Year: 2018

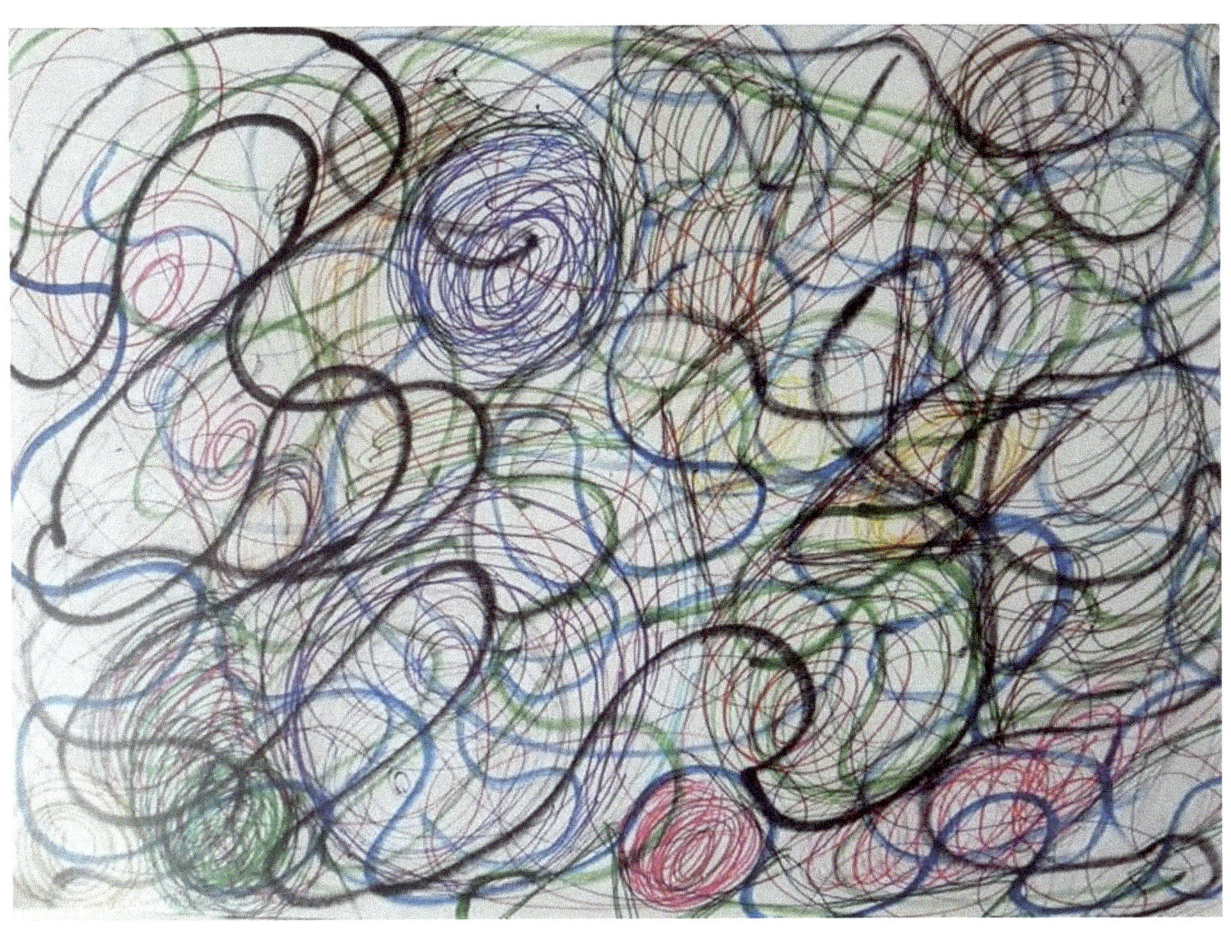

~~Unnamed 50~~
Mediums: markers, fibre ink pen and ball point pen ink on paper
Size: A3
Year: 2021

Mmap Multi-disciplinary Series

If you have enjoyed *The Aporia of Unnamed Things*, consider these other fine books in the **Mmap Multi-disciplinary Series** from *Mwanaka Media and Publishing:*

Africanization and Americanization Anthology Volume 1, Searching for Interracial, Interstitial, Intersectional and Interstates Meeting Spaces, Africa Vs North America by Tendai R Mwanaka
A Conversation..., A Contact by Tendai Rinos Mwanaka
Africa, UK and Ireland: Writing Politics and Knowledge Production Vol 1 by Tendai R Mwanaka
Writing Language, Culture and Development, Africa Vs Asia Vol 1 by Tendai R Mwanaka, Wanjohi wa Makokha and Upal Deb
Zimbolicious: An Anthology of Zimbabwean Literature and Arts, Vol 3 by Tendai Mwanaka
Drawing Without Licence by Tendai R Mwanaka
Writing Grandmothers/ Escribiendo sobre nuestras raíces: Africa Vs Latin America Vol 2 by Tendai R Mwanaka and Felix Rodriguez
Tiny Human Protection Agency by Megan Landman
Ghetto Symphony by Mandla Mavolwane

A Portrait of Defiance by Tendai Rinos Mwanaka
Nationalism: (Mis)Understanding Donald Trump's Capitalism, Racism, Global Politics, International Trade and Media Wars, Africa Vs North America Vol 2 by Tendai R Mwanaka
Ouafa and Thawra: About a Lover From Tunisia by Arturo Desimone
Zimbolicious: An Anthology of Zimbabwean Literature and Arts, Vol 4 by Tendai Mwanaka and Jabulani Mzinyathi
Chitungwiza Mushamukuru Anthology by Tendai Rinos Mwanaka
The Day and the Dweller: A Study of the Emerald Tablets by Jonathan Thompson
Zimbolicious: An Anthology of Zimbabwean Literature and Arts, Vol 5 by Tendai Mwanaka
Robotics Anthology, Africa vs Asia Vol 2 by Tendai Rinos Mwanaka
Shaping Up by Tendai Rinos Mwanaka
Zimbolicious Anthology Vol 6: An Anthology of Zimbabwean Literature and Arts by Tendai Rinos Mwanaka and Chenjerai Mhondera
Registers of Loss: PhotoTalking to the Baobab Trees of Nyatate by Tendai Rinos Mwanaka

The Trick is to Keep Breathing: Covid 19 Stories From African and North American Writers, vol 3 by Tendai Rinos Mwanaka
Fixing Earth: An Anthology of Ireland, UK and Africa Writers, Vol 2 by Tendai Rinos Mwanaka
Zimbolicious: An Anthology of Zimbabwean Literature and Arts, Vol 7 Tendai Rinos Mwanaka and Tanaka Chidora
Writing Woman Anthology: Personal Essays and Short stories, An Anthology of African and Asian Writers, Vol 3 by Tendai Rinos Mwanaka, Abigail George, Sue Zhu and Monalisa Jena
Writing Woman Anthology: Drama and Scholarly Essays, An Anthology of African and Asian Writers, Vol 3 by Tendai Rinos Mwanaka, Abigail George, Sue Zhu and Monalisa Jena
WRITING WOMAN ANTHOLOGY: Poetry and Visual art by Tendai Rinos Mwanaka, Abigail George, Sue Zhu and Monalisa Jena
Zimbolicious: An Anthology of Zimbabwean Literature and Arts, Vol 8 by Tendai Rinos Mwanaka and Matthew Kunashe Chikono
Of poets, gods, ghosts. Irritants and storytellers by Tendai Rinos Mwanaka

Upcoming

https://facebook.com/MwanakaMediaAndPublishing/

www.ingramcontent.com/pod-product-compliance
Lightning Source LLC
LaVergne TN
LVHW081253100826
845148LV00009B/1208

* 9 7 8 1 7 7 9 3 3 1 4 3 4 *